America's Greatest Engineering Project
Transcontinental Railroad, the Panama Canal

By Charles River Editors

Picture of the ceremony commemorating the completion of the Transcontinental Railroad

About Charles River Editors

Charles River Editors provides superior editing and original writing services across the digital publishing industry, with the expertise to create digital content for publishers across a vast range of subject matter. In addition to providing original digital content for third party publishers, we also republish civilization's greatest literary works, bringing them to new generations of readers via ebooks.

Introduction

The Transcontinental Railroad

Picture of the ceremony commemorating the completion of the Transcontinental Railroad

"The necessity that now exists for constructing lines of railroad and telegraphic communication between the Atlantic and Pacific coasts of this continent is no longer a question for argument; it is conceded by every one. In order to maintain our present position on the Pacific, we must have some more speedy and direct means of intercourse than is at present afforded by the route through the possessions of a foreign power." – 1856 report made by the Select Committee on the Pacific Railroad and Telegraph of the U.S. House of Representatives

The Transcontinental Railroad, laid across the United States during the 1860s, remains the very epitome of contradiction. On the one hand, it was a triumph of engineering skills over thousands of miles of rough terrain, but on the other hand, it drained the natural resources in those places nearly dry. It "civilized" the American West by making it easier for women and children to travel there, but it dispossessed Native American civilizations that had lived there for generations. It made the careers of many men and destroyed the lives from many others. It was bold and careless, ingenious and cruel, gentle and violent, and it enriched some and bankrupted others. In short, it was the best and worst of 19th century America in action.

As settlers pushed west and the Gold Rush brought an influx of Americans to California, the need for something like the Transcontinental Railroad was apparent to the government in the 1850s, and with the help of private companies, government officials conducted all kinds of land surveys in order to plot a course.

Of course, even once a route was chosen, the backbreaking work itself had to be done to connect railroad lines across the span of nearly 2,000 miles. This required an incredible amount of manpower, often consisting of unskilled laborers engaging in dangerous work, and the financial resources poured into it were also extreme. J. . O. Wilder, a Central Pacific-Southern Pacific employee, described a typical scene: "The Chinese were as steady, hard-working a set of men as could be found. With the exception of a few whites at the west end of Tunnel No. 6, the laboring force was entirely composed of Chinamen with white foremen and a 'boss/translator'. A single foreman (often Irish) with a gang of 30 to 40 Chinese men generally constituted the force at work at each end of a tunnel; of these, 12 to 15 men worked on the heading, and the rest on the bottom, removing blasted material. When a gang was small or the men were needed elsewhere, the bottoms were worked with fewer men or stopped so as to keep the headings going."

Ultimately, the project was considered so important that work on it progressed throughout the Civil War, and it took the better part of the 1860s before it was finally completed. Once the railroad was in place, it proved a boon to building up the American West, especially the Southwest and Pacific Northwest in places like Nevada, Utah, Wyoming, Colorado, Oregon and Washington.

The Panama Canal

The USS *Missouri* in the Panama Canal in 1945

"While the rights of sovereignty of the States occupying this region (Central America) should always be respected, we shall expect that these rights be exercised in a spirit befitting the occasion and the wants and circumstances that have arisen. Sovereignty has its duties as well as its rights, and none of these local governments, even if administered with more regard to the just demands of other nations than they have been, would be permitted, in a spirit of Eastern isolation, to close the gates of intercourse on the great highways of the world, and justify the act by the pretension that these avenues of trade and travel belong to them and that they choose to shut them, or, what is almost equivalent, to encumber them with such unjust relations as would prevent their general use." - United States Secretary of State Lewis Cass, 1858

Most people have heard of the Seven Wonders of the Ancient World, but while not as many have heard of the Seven Wonders of the Modern World, those who have are aware that the Panama Canal is considered one of them. In a world where few natural rivers carved out over eons of time have reached a length of more than 50 miles, the idea that a group of men could carve a canal of that length seemed impossible. In fact, many thought it could not be done.

On the other hand, there was a tremendous motivation to try, because if a canal could be successfully cut across Central America to connect the Atlantic and Pacific Oceans, it would cut weeks off the time necessary to carry goods by sea from the well-established East Coast of the United States to the burgeoning West Coast. Moreover, traveling around the tip of South America was fraught with danger, and European explorers and settlers had proposed building a canal in Panama or Nicaragua several centuries before the Panama Canal was actually built. By the late 19th century, the French actually tried to build such a canal, only to fail after a great deal of resources were put into construction and after workers died of malaria and other illnesses.

At the turn of the 20th century, not only was the need for a canal still there, but the right man was in the White House. Indeed, President Theodore Roosevelt, a celebrated outdoorsman, might have been the only president who could have foreseen and accomplished such an audacious feat, and even he considered it one of his crowning achievements. He wrote in his memoirs, "There are plenty of other things I started merely because the time had come that whoever was in power would have started them. But the Panama Canal would not have started if I had not taken hold of it, because if I had followed the traditional or conservative method I should have submitted an admirable state paper to Congress…the debate would be proceeding at this moment…and the beginning of work on the canal would be fifty years in the future. Fortunately [the opportunity] came at a period when I could act unhampered. Accordingly I took the Isthmus, started the canal and then left Congress not to debate the canal, but to debate me."

Building the Panama Canal was a herculean task in every sense. Taking about 10 years to build, workers had to excavate millions of cubic yards of earth and fight off hordes of insects to make Roosevelt's vision a reality. Roosevelt also had to tie up the U.S. Navy in a revolt in Colombia to ensure Panama could become independent and thus ensure America had control of the canal. By 1914, ships were finally traversing through the Panama Canal, just as World War I was about to start, and a century later, the Panama Canal remains one of the world's most vital waterways.

The Hoover Dam

1904 picture of the site before the Hoover Dam

"This morning I came, I saw, and I was conquered, as everyone would be who sees for the first time this great feat of mankind…Ten years ago the place where we gathered was an unpeopled, forbidding desert. In the bottom of the gloomy canyon whose precipitous walls rose to height of more than a thousand feet, flowed a turbulent, dangerous river…The site of Boulder City was a cactus-covered waste. And the transformation wrought here in these years is a twentieth century marvel." – President Franklin D. Roosevelt, September 30, 1935

During the 1930s, at the height of the Great Depression, thousands of workers began work on the Hoover Dam, built in the Black Canyon, which had been cut by the powerful Colorado River. The Colorado River was responsible for the Grand Canyon, and by the 20th century, the idea of damming the river and creating an artificial lake was being explored for all of its potential, including hydroelectric power and irrigation. By the time the project was proposed in the 1920s, the contractors vowing to build it were facing the challenge of building the largest dam the world had ever known. As if that wasn't enough, the landscape was completely unforgiving, as described by the famous explorer John Wesley Powell generations earlier: "The landscape everywhere, away from the river, is of rock--cliffs of rock, tables of rock, plateaus of rock, terraces of rock, crags of rock--ten thousand strangely carved forms…cathedral shaped buttes, towering hundreds or thousands of feet, cliffs that cannot be scaled, and canyon walls that shrink the river into insignificance, with vast hollow domes and tall pinnacles and shafts set on the verge overhead; and all highly colored."

The engineering that went into the Hoover Dam was not just dangerous but unprecedented, to the extent that the Hoover Dam relied on building methods that had never been proven effective on such a giant scale. The project also had to employ tens of thousands of people in often dangerous working conditions, which resulted in scores of deaths. At the same time, however, the large number of men that traveled to work on the project helped turn Las Vegas, a nearby small desert town in Nevada, into Sin City.

Despite all the difficulties, the Hoover Dam was completed on time, and President Roosevelt summed up just how impressive the accomplishment was in his speech dedicating the site in 1935: "We are here to celebrate the completion of the greatest dam in the world, rising 726 feet above the bedrock of the river and altering the geography of a whole region: we are here to see the creation of the largest artificial lake in the world-115 miles long, holding enough water, for example, to cover the whole State of Connecticut to a depth of ten feet; and we are here to see nearing completion a power house which will contain the largest generators and turbines yet installed in this country, machinery that can continuously supply nearly two million horsepower of electric energy."

America's Greatest Engineering Projects: The Construction History of the Transcontinental Railroad, the Panama Canal, and the Hoover Dam chronicles the construction of each major project, and their subsequent history. Along with pictures of important people, places, and events, you will learn about the Transcontinental Railroad, Panama Canal, and Hoover Dam like never before.

The Transcontinental Railroad

This Was Going to Make Money

"In July of 1860, California is a different world than it was…the previous October. Everybody is trying to get to Virginia City, Nevada. The Comstock was discovered in late 1859. California had basically been in a depression for five years. The gold rush had been over. And suddenly there's silver just across the mountains. And there's this huge rush from California to Virginia City. And people are beginning to think that they could build a railroad to Virginia City. There's suddenly financial incentive to build directly into the Sierra. So many places in the Sierra Nevada, there's a double summit. You come across the mountains and you drop down into a valley such as the valley where Lake Tahoe is. And then on the other side, you got another mountain ridge that you have to cross. And at Donner, you've only got one Summit. You come up the American River, you go down the Truckee River. And by being on the ridge above the river, you have a nice continuous plain that you use as a ramp. He knew that this was going to be a shortcut to Virginia City. This was going to make money." - Historian Wendell Huffman

At the time the Transcontinental Railroad was first proposed, it seemed impossible that more than 2,000 miles of steel track, representing the latest and greatest in transportation, could be laid across North America. What was perhaps most amazing was that, at the time it was built, there were basically no American settlements between its two destinations: the Missouri and the Sacramento Rivers. In fact, according to Joseph C. G. Kennedy, the Superintendent of the 1860 Census, "Previous to 1850 by far the greater portion of railroads constructed were in the States bordering the Atlantic, and ... were for the most part isolated lines, whose limited traffics were altogether local. ... [T]he internal commerce of the country was conducted almost entirely through water lines, natural and artificial, and over ordinary highways. The period of settlement of California marks really the commencement of the new era in the physical progress of the United States. The vast quantities of gold it produced imparted new life and activity to every portion of the Union, particularly the western States, the people of which, at the commencement of 1850, were thoroughly aroused as to the value and importance of railroads." Indeed, by the time the project was finished, hundreds of railroad towns, some of which would become America's biggest cities, had sprung up along its path.

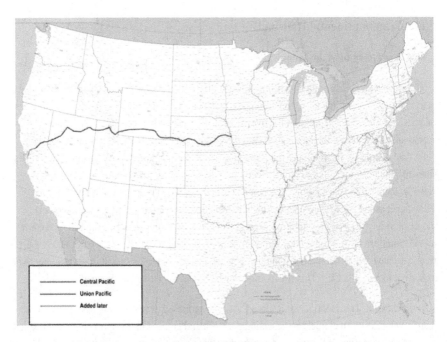

Map of the route

Picture of the burgeoning town of Cheyenne, Wyoming in the wake of the railroad

At the same time, it seemed impossible to imagine not having a Transcontinental Railroad eventually. Less than 40 years earlier, President James Monroe formulated the doctrine that would bear his name when he announced in 1823 that "as a principle in which the rights and interests of the United States are involved, that the American continents, by the free and independent condition which they have assumed and maintain, are henceforth not to be considered as subjects for future colonization by any European powers..." And yet, if Europe was not going to make use of America's vast wilderness and seemingly endless resources, who would? Obviously the ever-expanding United States. Thus, the Monroe Doctrine helped give rise to Manifest Destiny, the belief on the part of 19th century Americans that it was both their right and their responsibility to settle the west. Manifest Destiny, in turn, gave rise to the Transcontinental Railroad.

It is probably no coincidence that Theodore Judah, the man who would see the railroad go from dream to reality, was born in 1826 and came of age when steam power was a new marvel. While he was still in school, he heard tales that the new carriage pulled along tracks by steam engines could someday make their way across the entire continent from sea to shining sea. Asa Whitney, one of the first men to lobby for such a railroad, proclaimed, "[W]e shall have the whole world tributary to us—when the whole commerce of the vast world will be tumbled into our lap—when this vast and now useless waste and wilderness (and it ever must be so, without this road) shall become, not only the thoroughfare of the vast world, but its garden, feeding, clothing, comforting and enlightening millions, who are now starving, homeless, naked, ignorant and oppressed; and who can oppose such a work?"

Judah

Whitney

At the time, however, not everyone was convinced that there was even anything worth travelling to in the West. For example, in 1843, Senator George McDuffie of South Carolina asserted, "The whole region beyond the Rocky mountains and a vast tract between that chain and the Mississippi is a desert, without value for agricultural purposes, and which no American citizen should be compelled to inhabit unless as a punishment for crime. ... I would not for that [agricultural] purpose give a pinch of snuff for the whole territory. I wish to God we did not own it. I wish it was an impassable barrier to secure us from the intrusion of others. This is the character of the country. Who are we going to send there? Do you think your honest farmers in Pennsylvania, New York, or even in Ohio and Missouri, will abandon their farms to go upon any such enterprise as this? God forbid, if any man is to go to that country under the temptation of this bill? ... If I had a son who was a fit subject for Botany Bay (an Australian penal colony), I would urge him to go there."

Over a generation earlier, however, young Zebulon Pike had a far different impression. Pike may not be as famous as Lewis and Clark, but President Thomas Jefferson had him lead an expedition to explore the southern portion of the Louisiana Purchase, and he wrote of his travels in the West: "This area in time might become as celebrated as the African deserts. In various places [there were] tracts of many leagues, where the wind had thrown up the sand in all the fanciful forms of the ocean's rolling wave, and on which not a spear of vegetable matter existed."

Pike

The main barrier to reaching California at the time was the distance and lack of proper transportation. It took five hard, miserable, and often deadly months to travel 2,000 miles to California, much of it over desert and past the many graves of those who had gone before and not made it. It is no surprise, then, that while later settlers would move west in family groups, most of those who first made the long trek to California were single men.

The men who went to California and those who built the railroad to get them there had one driving force in common: gold. One of the most important and memorable events of the United States' westward push across the frontier came with the discovery of gold in the lands that became California in January 1848. Located thousands of miles away from the country's power centers on the East Coast at the time, the announcement came a month before the Mexican-American War had ended, and among the very few Americans that were near the region at the time, many of them were Army soldiers who were participating in the war and garrisoned there. San Francisco was still best known for being a Spanish military and missionary outpost during the colonial era, and only a few hundred called it home. Mexico's independence, and its possession of those lands, had come only a generation earlier.

Everything changed almost literally overnight. While the Mexican-American War technically concluded with a treaty in February 1948, the announcement brought an influx of an estimated 90,000 "Forty-Niners" to the region in 1849, hailing from other parts of America and even as far away as Asia. All told, an estimated 300,000 people would come to California over the next few years, as men dangerously trekked thousands of miles in hopes of making a fortune, and in a span of months, San Francisco's population exploded, making it one of the first mining boomtowns to truly spring up in the West. This was a pattern that would repeat itself across the West anytime a mineral discovery was made, from the Southwest and Tombstone to the Dakotas and Deadwood. Of course, that was made possible by the collective memory of the original California gold rush.

For the railroad developers, the Gold Rush was figurative gold, as the massive numbers of people heading west offered the promise of making a fortune in the newly developing train industry. Railroad executives successfully lobbied Congress to investigate the possibility of a "Pacific Railroad," and naturally, it wasn't hard to convince Congressmen anxious to bring trade and people to their respective districts to lobby for better transportation to their often under-populated territories. At the same time, like all good politicians, they were more interested in having the trains run through their states than where the railroad lines eventually ended.

Now Ready for the Iron

"It is but little over a year since the Pacific Railroad Bill was received in California. It was signed by the President on the 1st of July, 1862, and reached California in August following. Within the intervening time the company has obtained subscriptions to the stock for near nearly a million of dollars; sent an agent to the East who purchased the iron and rolling stock for seventy miles of the road, six hundred tons of which have arrived, while four thousand tons are known to be afloat; seventy-five miles of the road have been carefully surveyed and located, and thirty miles put under contract, eighteen of which is now ready for the iron; and, as before stated, a commencement to lay it down was made yesterday. Unless delayed by the failure of the iron to arrive, the eighteen miles will be in running condition before the first of December. The twelve more to make the thirty are under contract, to be completed on the 1st of January, 1864. During the winter, the locomotives and trains of the company will be running to the Thirty Mile Station." - *Sacramento Daily Union*

Constantly jockeying for position, America's leaders might have remained hopelessly deadlocked had Judah not arrived on the scene. A civil engineer, he had worked on railroads in both the east and California, and now he wanted to see them built in all parts in between.

Fortunately, Judah not only had practical building skills but also a talent for making people believe that something could be built. In 1859, he appealed to Congress for funding for a survey to determine if indeed a route could be found for the tracks, and, if so, where the best route might be. Given that the country was on the verge of the Civil War, he had little luck, so he pursued the project on his own and, in October 1860, found a comrade in Daniel Strong, a man very interested in bringing the railroad to his little town of Dutch Flat, California. He took Judah to the top of the Sierra Mountains and then showed him a place where they both agreed the tracks could make it through.

Once back in the valley, the two men formed the Central Pacific Railroad Company and began marketing their visions to anyone with deep pockets. One of the first men to come aboard was Collis P. Huntington, a wealthy hardware wholesaler, and Huntington brought along his business partner, Mark Hopkins, and Charles Crocker, a dry-goods merchant. Crocker in turn convinced his brother, E.B. Crocker, to invest, as well as Leland Stanford, later governor of California. Together the men raised about $150,000, not nearly enough to finance a railroad of any size, much less the size they were proposing, but it was enough money to sponsor a survey, which Judah completed in 1861.

Stanford

It would be impossible for Judah's timing to have been any worse. The country had already begun to splinter, with a number of Southern states seceding from the Union, and each new day brought increasingly worse news to Washington. Right into the middle of this maelstrom walked Judah, carrying with him a 60 foot long map of the proposed rail line. Setting up in the largest empty office space he could find, he entertained any Congressman that walked in, showing them drawings of bridges and tunnels, as well as water tanks and train depots. What Judah did not draw their attention to was the fact that the Sierra Mountains were more than 7,000 feet tall in some areas, and that they were often plagued by deep snow drifts and mud slides. He also neglected to mention that they would have to blow 18 tunnels, each of them hundreds of feet long, through solid granite and dig shelves into the side of sheer cliffs. Had he told them all these things, someone might have mentioned that there was not even a company on the West Coast of the United States that was large enough to produce the trains needed to cover such a vast expanse, or even the rails themselves.

However, one man believed in the dream, perhaps because he desperately needed something positive to work on. With the nation he had sworn "to preserve, protect and defend" splitting in two, he decided to throw money and political collateral into a project that he would ultimately never see completed. Of course, it didn't hurt that having easy transportation to California, Oregon and Nevada would help keep them, and their resources, securely in the Union and at his disposal. That is how President Abraham Lincoln came to sign a bill on July 1, 1862 that "created and erected into a body corporate and politic in deed and in lay, by the name, style, and title of 'The Union Pacific Railroad Company.'" The bill also mandated that "the said corporation is hereby authorized and empowered to layout, locate, construct, furnish, maintain, and enjoy a continuous railroad and telegraph, with the appurtenances...." To finance the venture, the government promised the company $48,000 and 6,400 acres of land per mile of track laid. To protect itself, the federal government would withhold 20% of the promised funds until the railroad was completed. If that did not take place within 12 years, the company would forfeit all its holdings to the government.

Thus, bright and early on January 8, 1863, the new Governor of California, Leland Stanford, stood in downtown Sacramento and ceremoniously dug a shiny new shovel into the cool, black soil, marking the beginning of construction on the Transcontinental Railroad. Around him were some of the leading families and politicians of the state, but after the fanfare died down, he and his partners were very alone and facing the daunting prospect of making an American dream come true. Their first job was to finish selling the stock necessary to raise the funds for the railroad, and they completed this by late September 1863, buoyed by public enthusiasm and a supportive press. One paper reported, "A few weeks since it was reported that all the stock of the Union Central Pacific Railroad had been subscribed, the ten percent paid in, and the company organized. This company is to build the road from the western line of Kansas to the eastern boundary of California. The law, however, provides that the Central California Pacific Railroad Company may continue to build east through Nevada and Utah Territories, in the event of their building their road to the east line of California before the Union Pacific Company reach that Point from the East with a railroad. The prospects now are that the California company will complete their road to the east line of the State before the Union Company finish theirs through Nebraska. In fact, the road must be built from the two ends: upon the center section little can be done until it can be reached by rail each way. Hence the vast importance of pushing the work at the east and west ends of the road as rapidly as possible. On this point we maintain that the Central California Pacific Railroad Company has accomplished more than could have been expected under the circumstances."

Picture of a Pacific Railroad Bond

After weeks of jostling about and trying to get many different contracts, the railroad company decided to take just one contract for the completion of the project, and to put Charles Crocker in charge of it. This bothered Judah, who did not trust the man, but at the same time, Judah never got along well with any of his fellow investors. This exacerbated problems with contractors Judah had previously hired, as well as Eastern companies he had contracted with to provide the iron for the project. Things finally came to a head in mid-1863 when Judah left California and returned to New York, probably hoping to find others who would help him buy back his company. Tragically, he never found those men because he contracted an illness during the trip and died in early November 1863.

Crocker

Had Judah lived just another week or two, he may have received word that the first rail had finally been laid in Sacramento on October 26. According to the *Sacramento Daily Union*, "Yesterday morning the contractor to build a section of eighteen miles laid the first rail on the western end of the Pacific Railroad...Quite a number of persons were present to witness the work, though no notice that it was to be done had been published. Those engaged in the enterprise did not choose to have any ceremony over the affair; they made a regular business matter of an event which in the eye of the public is the first certain step taken in building the great Pacific Railroad. Grading has been done, bridges built: but nothing looks to the public so much like making a railroad as the work of laying down the iron on the roadbed. On the Atlantic side the contract for building the section through Kansas has been let two or three times, but up to this date we have seen no report of rails laid, though not long since we saw it stated that a shipment of iron had been made from New York for the Kansas section. But no iron has yet been laid. The credit, therefore, of having put down the first rail on the line must be awarded to the California Central Pacific Railroad Company."

Then, a few weeks after the first western rail was laid, President Lincoln finally decided on the location of the eastern terminus of the railroad. It would be Council Bluffs, Iowa, a location that would prove to be a life-changing boon for a man named Dr. Thomas Clark Durant. Already the vice president of the Union Pacific Railroad Company, Durant was a consummate businessman who made most of his money off of real estate developed along the side of the tracks, which allowed him to quickly (and illegally) manage to take control of the company. Durant used funds he raised to bribe Congressmen into supporting the best interests of the railroad, and with full knowledge that the company would be paid by the mile by the government, he altered the proposed route of the tracks to change the railroad from a more or less straight line into a large curved pattern.

Durant

Since Durant was more interested in selling shares and making money than actually seeing track installed, more than a year passed without any real progress being made on the eastern end of the railroad. Once the Civil War ended, however, the distractions that kept Congress from watching what he was doing were mostly gone. Durant was finally compelled to implement a flurry of building, driving those under him to get busy building the railroad he had been telling people already existed.

Peasants of Kwangtung

Pictures of Chinese workers on the Central Pacific

"The peasants of Kwangtung were indentured in California to locally run Chinese district companies, signed on for up to five years of labor at comparatively low wages until their tickets were paid; they then filtered out into the streams and rivers of the Sierra slope in search of gold. Enforcement thugs and old-world penalties awaited slackers and deserters, but the life, hard as it was, promised rewards, particularly the hope that two or three hundred dollars could be amassed— enough by Kwangtung standards for a return home and a luxury retirement. Until that happy time, which rarely attended any of the immigrants, there were only the diversions of gambling, prostitution, and opium, establishments for which sprang up in the Chinatowns of San Francisco, Sacramento, Stockton, and Marysville, and in the smaller mountainside encampments beneath roofs of canvas." - David Haward Bain, author of *Empire Express: Building the First Transcontinental Railroad*

While things in the east were going in fits and starts, back on the West Coast, the Central Pacific line was having problems recruiting workers. Crocker had hired a determined boss named James Harvey Strobridge to drive the men, most of whom were recent immigrants from Ireland, but he could not put to work people who would not be hired. As a result, the company agreed to try something new by hiring Chinese immigrants, a move pushed heavily by Crocker, who once replied to Strobridge's objections by saying, "Did they not build the Chinese Wall, the biggest piece of masonry in the world?"

As Leland Stanford wrote in 1865, "A large majority of the white laboring class on the Pacific Coast find more profitable and congenial employment in mining and agricultural pursuits, than in railroad work. The greater portion of the laborers employed by us are Chinese, who constitute a large element in the population of California. Without them it would be impossible to complete the western portion of this great national enterprise, within the time required by the Acts of Congress. As a class they are quiet, peaceable, patient, industrious and economical—ready and apt to learn all the different kinds of work required in railroad building, they soon become as efficient as white laborers. More prudent and economical, they are contented with less wages. We find them organized into societies for mutual aid and assistance. These societies, that count their numbers by thousands, are conducted by shrewd, intelligent business men, who promptly advise their subordinates where employment can be found on the most favorable terms. No system similar to slavery, serfdom or peonage prevails among these laborers. Their wages, which are always paid in coin, at the end of each month, are divided among them by their agents, who attend to their business, in proportion to the labor done by each person. These agents are generally American or Chinese merchants, who furnish them their supplies of food, the value of which they deduct from their monthly pay. We have assurances from leading Chinese merchants, that under the just and liberal policy pursued by the Company, it will be able to procure during the next year, not less than 15,000 laborers. With this large force, the Company will be able to push on the work so as not only to complete it far within the time required by the Acts of Congress, but so as to meet the public impatience."

The flow of Chinese immigrants to the West Coast had started in earnest over a decade earlier, sparked in large part by a crop failure in southern China that caused the custom houses in San Francisco to swell with 20,026 Chinese arrivals. Even more Chinese came as news reached China about the apparent ease of mining in California. By the end of the decade, ⅛ of the population of the Southern Mines consisted of Chinese miners, and they would become known as the most industrious and tireless of the miners, finding gold in claims that previous owners had thought depleted and persisting in mining an area far longer than others who eventually left the fields altogether.

However, other miners reacted to their presence negatively, and in some cases Chinese miners had their camps violently attacked. The state government attempted to rectify the problem through the creation of a second Miner's Tax, but unfortunately this only seemed to accelerate other miners' attacks on Chinese camps. Reports in the same year indicated that an epidemic of robberies hit the immigrant miners from China, close to 200 alone, along with a series of murders.

All of this partly explains why the Chinese decided to diversify and choose occupations that did not put them into open competition with white American miners. Another reason, and one closer to the financial windfalls that occurred during the Gold Rush, is explained by the chance for profit in the mercantile and service industries. The Chinese moved into the laundry business, other domestic services, and later railroad building, all of which necessarily thrived as the population in the region boomed.

Word soon reached the Kwangtung province that America was hiring many men to build its new railroad, and after years of famine, many Chinese families needed a new start. Thus, Chinese men began flooding into California to seek fortunes not in gold but in shiny iron rails, and by 1866, 80% of the West Coast railroad workforce was made up of Chinese immigrants. In 1867, author Albert Richardson wrote, "The cars now run nearly to the summit of the Sierras. At the time of my visit the terminus was Colfax, fifty-five miles east of Sacramento. Thence we took horses for twelve miles. Upon this little section of road four thousand laborers were at work—one-tenth Irish, the rest Chinese. They were a great army laying siege to Nature in her strongest citadel. The rugged mountains looked like stupendous ant-hills. They swarmed with Celestials, shoveling, wheeling, carting, drilling and blasting rocks and earth, while their dull, moony eyes stared out from under immense basket-hats, like umbrellas. At several dining camps we saw hundreds sitting on the ground, eating soft boiled rice with chopsticks as fast as terrestrials could with soup-ladles. Irish laborers received thirty dollars per month (gold) and board; Chinese, thirty-one dollars, boarding themselves. After a little experience the latter were quite as efficient and far less troublesome. The Hudson Bay Company in its balmy days was compelled to import laborers from the Sandwich Islands; and without the Chinese the California end of the great national thoroughfare must have been delayed for many years. Twelve thousand are now employed upon it."

A picture of Chinese workers

Union Pacific Railroad construction

Courtesy of Wyoming State Archives

A picture of Irish workers

Coming from a culture known for its grace and acrobatic feats, the men proved to be natural for carving out narrow shelves into the granite walls of the Sierra Mountains. They would be lowered by ropes tied around trees and, once in position, drill into the side of the mountain, filling the holes they created with black powder and a fuse they hoped was long enough to allow them to get back to the top of the mountain before it blew. As E.B. Crocker wrote, "The rock is full of seams. The men work the earth out of the seams with long hooked Iron rods, & then a keg or so of powder is fixed in them, which cleans out & opens the seam. Then 10 to 20 kegs are put in & the explosion sends the rock flying clear & out of the way."

However, as their reputation as hard workers spread, so did their popularity. In 1867, Crocker complained, "We have proved their value as laborers, and everybody is trying Chinese and now we can't get them." Though Crocker raised their pay to more than a dollar a day, good money at the time, the men soon realized that they could do better and went on strike on June 25 of that year. A few days later, Crocker said with pride, speaking at a Fourth of July picnic, that when one man told him, "Eight hours a day good for white man; all the same good for Chinaman," he disagreed and refused to shorten their 10 hour days. Still, he admitted privately to his brother, E.B., that, "This strike of the chinamen is the hardest blow we have had here. If we get over this without yielding, it will be all right hereafter." He also later wrote, "If there had been that number of white laborers... it would have been impossible to control them," Crocker would later recall. "But this strike of the Chinese was just like Sunday all along the work. These men stayed in their camps. That is, they would come out and walk around, but not a word was said. No violence was perpetrated along the whole line."

Determined to break the strike, Charles Crocker decided to stop importing food for the workers. At that point, according to E.B., "Their agents stopped supplying them with goods and provisions, and they really began to suffer. None of us went near them for a week— did not want to exhibit anxiety. Then Charles went up, and they gathered around him—and he told them that he would not be dictated to— that he made the rules for them and not they for him. That if they went to work immediately they would remit the fines usually retained out of their wages when they did not work, but if they refused, he would pay them nothing for June. They tried hard to get some change, as to the hours for a day's work, or an advance of even 25 ¢ per month. Not a cent more would he give. The great majority gave right up when he was firm, a few threatened to whip those who went to work and burn their camps— but Charley told them that he would protect them & his men would shoot down any man that attempted to do the laborers any injury. He had the sheriff & posse come up to see that there was no fighting."

This marked the end of the strike, and as E.B. reported shortly after, "Since the strike the men are working hard & steady. There is a rush of chinamen on the work— most of the fresh arrivals from China go straight up to the work. It is all life & animation on the line [working] ...thick as bees."

Unfortunately, the company's problems, and those of their Chinese workers, were far from over. The winter of 1867-68 was a bad one, and according to one of the men who worked for the railroad at that time, "Most of the Chinese came to Truckee and they filled up all the old buildings and sheds that were in Truckee. With the heavy fall of snow the old barn collapsed and killed four Chinese. A good many were frozen to death. There was a dance at Donner Lake at a hotel, and a sleigh load of us went up from Truckee and on our return, about 9 A.M. next morning, we saw something under a tree by the side of the road, its shape resembling that of a man. We stopped and found a frozen Chinese. As a consequence, we threw him in the sleigh with the rest of us, and took him into town and laid him out by the side of a shed and covered him with a rice mat."

An Indian Fire

"Through the biting night air we were whirled down the eastern slope for three miles to Donner Lake, blue, shining, and sprinkled with stars, while from the wooded hill beyond glared an Indian fire like a great fiendish eyeball. The lake is an exquisite body of water, though less impressive than Tahoe; and the reflections of snowy peak, pine forest, clear sky, and minute twig and leaf in its depths, seem almost miraculous. The illustration, as faithful to nature as artist and engraver can make it, is far less vivid than the original photograph. In that, concealing the boat, figures and trees in the foreground-water, it is almost impossible to decide which side up the picture should be—which are the real hills, snow and forest, and which the reflection." - Albert Richardson, author of *Beyond the Mississippi*

Back east, Durant found himself with plenty of men looking for work, most of them recently discharged veterans of the Civil War, and to govern and direct these recent veterans, he hired General Grenville Dodge, a former Union commander in the Great Plains. He also hired Jack and Dan Casement, two brothers with extensive experience in railroad construction, but during the winter he spent in Omaha, Jack Casement often found himself plagued by concerns about his wife Francis, whom he had left back in Ohio. Their four year old son had recently passed away, and she was having a difficult time bearing the loss. At one point, she wrote to Jack, "When I go to bed here all alone I think so much about Charlie and I see his little pale face while he lay sick, then his little body as he lay in his coffin and then that little mound of earth. I have never missed Charlie so much since he died as I have since you left me. I love you dearly and it is so hard for me to live away from you." To this, Jack replied, "I am first rate but impatient to have the ice go out of the river. It is mighty lonesome here and I am impatient to get to work. I want to see the thing start before I leave here. Just as soon as I get a bar laid I mean to travel home for my true love."

Dodge

The cold, both physical and mental, continued to plague the couple, as Francis wrote, "How many lonesome Sundays I have had in the past five years and I suppose I must expect more if I live. This cold weather does not look much like opening up the river, does it? I am trying to be patient, but it is rather hard." But life, and the job, went on, and Jack was finally able to report, "The river is beginning to rise. I have been working with a few men grading and putting in a side track. We will commence track-laying next Monday."

Jack and Francis

While the railroad proved to be a boon for one culture, it spelled the death knell for another. Prior to the coming of the railroad, it was still possible that Anglo-Saxon immigration to the West might be slow enough to allow the new white families to live peacefully alongside their Native American neighbors. However, the railroad, even at the time of its construction, opened the floodgates of settlement and quickly drove tribes in the West further off their land. On January 9, 1866, the Superintendent Indian Affairs in Carson City, Nevada, wrote that "the lands not occupied by [the Indians] (and which are producing nothing) are the best farming lands on this portion of the State, and which would at once be settled by whites and cultivated, if an opportunity offered ... The rapid construction of the Pacific railroad, running as it will directly through these reservations, will necessarily consume the greater portion of the timber, as well as scatter the Indians from their present location. I cannot too strongly urge upon the department the necessity of an early removal of these Indians..."

With their homes and lands threatened, the Native Americans fought back in both small groups and large ones. On June 22, 1867, *Harper's Weekly* reported, "Operations on the Smoky Hill and Arkansas routes have ceased for the present, and the attention of General Sherman had been devoted to the Platte River route. At Omaha, on June 8, he issued general orders stating that the Union Pacific Railroad shall be so well guarded in the future that no Indians will dare to interfere with it. All passengers and freight must be forwarded to the end of the tracks, and from there will be guarded by sufficient escorts specially provided for that purpose. He expressed himself as sanguine that he will clear the Platte Valley of Indians within two weeks. He had also, with the concurrence of Secretary Stanton, agreed to allow Governor Hunt, of Colorado, to equip five hundred volunteers for Indian service."

That same year, the Acting Commissioner for Indian Affairs wrote, "The steady growth of emigration to the grounds heretofore devoted to the chase and the rapid progress of railroads pointing towards the Pacific and traversing the country over which the Indians from time immemorial have roamed, imperiously demand that the policy of concentrating them upon reservations should, whenever practicable, be adopted. Until recently there was territory enough to supply the demands of the white race, without unduly encroaching upon the districts where the Indians subsisted by hunting. This condition of things no longer exists."

Then, just a few months later on November 16, 1867, there seemed to be some sort of breakthrough. Again, *Harper's Weekly* carried the story: "A peace which might have been as readily arranged two years ago as at present was made with four of the tribes of Indians of the Plains in October at an Indian camp on Medicine Lodge Creek, Kansas. By its terms the location of the reservations of the Kiowas, Comanches, Apaches, and Cheyennes are changed and enlarged. The tribes are to remove farther south -- that is, away from the line in the Kansas branch of the Pacific Railroad, and are not to disturb the laborers on that route. ... The full terms of the treaty give to each Indian on the reservation annually a suit of clothes, consisting of coat, pantaloons, hat, and socks, and in addition to this, $35,000 annually, in such articles as the Indians most need is to be given to the several tribes. Several other provisions are made to furnish seeds and agricultural implements to such Indians as may commence farming. The Indians agree to let all the railroads be built, and especially the Smoky Hill and Platte roads. They also agree to keep lasting peace; to capture no women or children; to attack no more trains, and to cease killing men; and it is also agreed to allow them to hunt on the old reservation, south of Arkansas, until the settlements drive them away from that hunting-ground."

The peace treaty, such as it was, was broken by the time the ink dried on the paper. While it is easy from the comfort of the 21st century to judge the behavior of either side, in the moment that events were unfolding, it was ultimately a life and death struggle for both sides. One railroad engineer recalled, "On leaving Sidney, [Nebraska] I opened the side door of the baggage car nearest the bluffs, threw down a trunk at the door and sat down. All at once, 'Bang'—there was an arrow sticking in the trunk between my legs just about six inches too low to get me. I didn't wait for the second arrow to come, but closed the door, went over to the locker where we kept about fifteen Spencer rifles to use in case of attack, took out a Spencer which was loaded, pushed the door open just far enough to stick out the end of the rifle and let go all the shot that was in it."

Soon, the train whistle itself became a sort of call to arms for the Cheyenne warriors, one of whom explained, "We said among ourselves, now the white people have taken all we had, we are to do something…The railroad is death to us, when the people hear the sound of the bell of the iron horse they mourn; it is the signal that the life they have known is over." Unfortunately, the warriors had good reason to be afraid, since even those whites who were not trying deliberately to wipe out the tribes managed to do it by spreading disease and consuming buffalo, the natives' primary food source. This situation was exacerbated during particularly difficult winters, and while many elder tribal leaders continued to try to negotiate some sort of peace agreement with the white leaders, the younger men in the tribes became increasingly angry and inclined to fight. At this point, the railroad reached out to the famous Civil War General William Tecumseh Sherman, notorious across the South for his Atlanta Campaign, March to the Sea, and the burning of Columbia, South Carolina.

Sherman proved to be as hostile toward the Native Americans as he had ever been toward his own countrymen: "The more we can kill this year the less will have to be killed the next year, for the more I see of these Indians the more convinced I am that they all have to be killed or be maintained as a species of paupers. ... We are not going to let a few thieving, ragged Indians check and stop the progress of the railroads.... I regard the railroad as the most important element now in progress to facilitate the military interests of our Frontier. We must act with vindictive earnestness against the Sioux, even to their extermination, men, women and children. (The Sioux must) feel the superior power of the Government. During an assault, the soldiers cannot pause to distinguish between male and female, or even discriminate as to age."

Sherman

Later, Casement wrote his wife, "The Indians are on the Rampage, killing and stealing all along the line. We don't apprehend any danger from them [because] our gang is so large. … We are now Sailing, and mean to lay over three miles every day." Casement had bragging rights now, as he was the leader of the team making this amazing progress. Still, author Albert Richardson pointed out, "Indians have thrown one or two trains off the track, but in general have kept very clear of the locomotive. In Kansas, however, they have committed many outrages. Going to California in 1867, via the Kansas Pacific road, and thence by stage through Denver and Salt Lake, was a hazardous undertaking. Near Fort Wallace, one day in June, a coach which carried five passengers, one soldier and a driver, had a running fight for five miles, with a hundred mounted Sioux and Cheyenne. The travelers made the best resistance they could with their rifles, and kept the savages at a little distance, while the driver put his horses to their utmost speed. Every man on board, except one, was killed or seriously wounded. An old frontier friend of mine, Charles H. Blake, happily escaped though with a broken arm and a wound in the head. At last the vehicle, with its bleeding and dying inmates, reached the shelter of Big Timbers Station, and the savages sullenly retired without having taken a single scalp. The fight was probably one of the last, and certainly one of the most remarkable in the history of the Plains."

Hell on Wheels

"In a giddy month or two the town would bulge with more than three hundred permanent structures and a number of temporary ones, such as a mammoth tent erected next to Miller's trading post by a man named McDonald, who furnished it with a bar, billiard tables, and gambling devices. And it would be McDonald who would endure the most competition. Each arriving train brought more camp followers to North Platte, and it became easier to find a drink of whiskey than a drink of water. Saloons and more saloons, dice and roulette parlors, and houses (and tents) of prostitution proliferated. Day and night the streets were jammed with drunken railroaders, prostitutes, pimps, pickpockets, and card sharks— but no lawmen. Winter snows arrived in December and if anything North Platte heated up. In the spring, when the end of track would be pushed farther west and the laborers moved on, the camp followers would simply fold up their tents, dismantle their gimcrack structures, crate their whiskey and corral their women, and ship them out to the new end of track to start up all over again. It was Samuel

Bowles of upright Springfield, Massachusetts, who would look at the scene, appalled and outraged, and give it an immortal name: 'Hell on Wheels.'" - Historian David Bain

By the summer of 1866, the men working their way west had become a well-oiled machine built around long days, loud nights, and military style discipline. The food was basic and not very good, but most of them had become accustomed to worse in the army or the starving villages of Ireland. Their one source of entertainment was Hell On Wheels, a sort of portable town that moved along with the railroad and offered gambling, drinking and prostitution. W. O. Owen, one the workers, described it: "It cost a man about $10 an hour to trip the light fantastic with those soiled doves, and if he had anything left they would drug him and strip him of everything of any value before kicking him into the street. Immediately in front of Bull's Big Tent occurred the first murder I ever witnessed. In 10 minutes after that shot was fired the excitement had subsided. The street was clear, the games were in full blast, and the cry of "Promenade to the bar!" was issuing from the Big Tent."

Henry Morgan Stanley, sent by the *St. Louis Missouri-Democrat* to report on the Great Plains, wrote, "The prairie around seemed turned into a canvas city…. Every gambler in the Union seems to have steered his course for North Platte, and every known game under the sun is played here. The days of Pike's Peak and California are revived. Every house is a saloon, and every saloon is a gambling den. Revolvers are in great requisition. Beardless youths imitate to the life the peculiar swagger of the devil-may-care bull-whacker and blackleg, and here, for the first time, they try their hands at the 'Mexican Monte,' 'high-low-jack,' 'strap,' 'rouge-et-noir,' 'three-card monte,' and that satanic game, 'chuck -a-luck,' and lose their all. 'Try again, my buck; nothing like 'sperience; you are cuttin' your eye-teeth now; by-and-by you will be a pioneer.' Such are the encouraging words shouted to an unfortunate young man by the sympathizing bystanders. On account of the immense freighting done to Idaho, Montana, Utah, Dakota, and Colorado, hundreds of bull-whackers walk about, and turn the one street into a perfect Babel. Old gamblers who reveled in the glorious days of 'flush times' in the gold districts, declare that this town outstrips all yet."

Obviously, the wives and mothers back home read these articles and became increasingly concerned about the moral and spiritual welfare of the men, even as they had already for so long been concerned about their physical welfare. Francis Casement wrote to her husband on November 25 to "get home as soon as possible— and darling be careful of your health— and for the sake of our little boy more for your own sake, beware of the tempter in the form of strong drink. There, I thought I was going through with this letter without a mention of that— but I can't help it now." However, Jack had bigger plans, replying, "Here it is almost Christmas and I am still here. And if I get home on New Year's now I shall feel thankful. There is so much to do. We want two or three hundred cows for next summer, are building a large ice house, have built a good slaughter house and Blacksmith shop, wash house and corral, so you see we are getting quite a ranch. Darling be as patient as you can. You don't want to see me more than I do you."

No matter what Mrs. Casement thought, the biggest threat to both the men and their progress was not liquor but snow. This was especially true for those approaching the track from the west. Engineer John R. Gillis later wrote, "About thirty feet from our windows was a large warehouse. This was often hidden completely by the furious torrent of almost solid snow that swept through the gorge. On the cliff above, the cedar trees are deeply cut, many branches of the thickness of a man's wrist being taken off entirely by the drifting snow-flakes. No one can face these storms when they are in earnest. Three of our party came through the pass one evening, walking with the storm— two got in safely. After waiting a while, just as we were starting out to look up the third, he came in exhausted. In a short, straight path between two walls of rock, he had lost his way and thought his last hour had come."

Avalanches were also a danger that often buried entire teams of workers. One worker noted that after one such event, "a man coming up the road missed the house and alarmed the camp, so that by six o'clock the men were dug out. The bulk of the slide had passed over and piled itself up beyond the house, so that it was only covered fifteen feet deep. Only three were killed; the bunks were close to the log walls and kept the rest from being crushed. The snow packed around the men so closely that only two could move about; they had almost dug their way out; over the heads of the rest little holes had been melted in the snow by their breath. Most of them were conscious, and, strange to say, the time had passed rapidly with them, although about fourteen hours under the snow."

In some ways, the aftermath of an avalanche was worse than the event itself, because once it was over, the men were faced with the daunting challenge of spending hundreds of work hours getting back to the place they had been before. According to Gilliss, the powdery snow was often waist deep, and "[i]nto this, the oxen would flounder, and when they lay down, worn out, be roused by the summary process of twisting their tails. I saw three in one team so fortunate as to have had theirs twisted clear off, none left to be bothered with. The men were as regardless of themselves as of their animals. They took life easily in fine weather, but were out nearly all the time when it stormed. Late at night they could be seen shoveling on a bad drift at the corner of the warehouse, where the wind heaped in the snow faster than they could dig it out, and then a denser mass of flying snow would hide them altogether."

Chinese workers in the snow

A snow gallery built in 1868 to protect workers and the railroad from the elements

The safest place to work during the winter was obviously inside the mountains rather than on them, and to that end, crews of men worked 24 hours a day blasting through mountains throughout the winter of 1866-67. According to historian David Bain, "The Summit Tunnel was 1,659 feet long and it's through some of the hardest rock in North America. And remember that we're working with hand drills and black blasting powder. It's not very efficient. It takes a lot of human effort and a lot of money to pay for that blasting powder." Even with their best efforts, the men were only cutting through about one foot of mountain per day and anticipating using up more than a year of precious time and resources to complete the tunnel.

All the while, Casement and his crew were moving toward them at what seemed to be the surprising speed of three or more miles per day. Each company, the Central Pacific from the west and the Union Pacific from the east, would control whatever line it completed, so progress mattered to both. As a result, the desperate men controlling the company took the calculated risk of authorizing the use of nitroglycerin to blast into the mountainside. Powerful but unstable, it had to be transported with the utmost care. To make its use as safe as possible, Crocker brought James Howden all the way from England just to mix the product on sight. Once there, he was able to use it to significantly speed up the blasting process.

A modern picture of the Summit Tunnel from The Cooper Collection of US Railroad History

Force as Was Necessary

"I immediately wired back to General J. S. Casement, telling him to take such of his force as was necessary and go back to Julesburg and clean the town out and hold it until the citizens there were willing to obey the orders of the officers I had placed in charge and pay for their lots. This was fun for Casement. I did not hear anything more in relation to what he had done there. When I saw him later, he said, 'I will show you what I did.'… He took me to a hill where there was quite a burial ground and he said, 'General, they all died in their boots and Julesburg has been quiet since.'" - Grenville Dodge

Before his death, President Lincoln had asked a Massachusetts Congressman named Oakes Ames to take control of the Union Pacific Railroad, apparently out of concern that Durant would run it into the ground. Ames finally completed his takeover during the summer of 1867 and made his brother, Oliver, the president of the company. Oliver Ames later wrote Dodge that his brother's success "has raised the very devil in that amiable Gent, & he has come down upon us with injunctions and proposes to visit us with every form of Legal Document to keep us honest. Such a lover of honesty and fair open dealing can't bear to see the money of the U.P.R.R. wasted on such scoundrels as make up the balance of the Board of Directors. I cannot understand such a change as has come over the Dr. The man of all others who has from the beginning stole wherever he had a chance & who is to-day we think holding stock and a large portion of his stock on fictitious claims and trumped up [accounts]. He is now in open hostility to the Road and any orders he may give you or any parties under you should be entirely disregarded."

Oakes Ames

While Durant resisted their efforts by every legal (and probably a few illegal) means possible, he eventually had to concede that they had won. From that point on, the three men were able to work together, and it didn't hurt that Durant soon learned that both the Ames' were just as inclined to grease palms in Congress as he was.

Bribery continued to be the order of the day back in the "civilized" east, but the workers in the west had bigger concerns, most notably prostitution and murder. It may be hard today to imagine a place where there are literally no laws, and no attempts to make or keep them, but this was the case in many of the towns popping up in the wake of the railroad. Speaking of one such town, Samuel Reed, a traveler passing through, wrote to his wife, "Julesburg continues to grow with magic rapidity, and vice and crime stalk unblushingly in the midday sun. General Augur and staff returned here last Friday evening and nothing would do but they must see the town by gas light. I sent for Dan Casement to pilot us (I knew he could show us the sights). The first place that we visited was a dance house, where a fresh importation of strumpets had been received. The hall was crowded with bad men and lewd women. Such profanity, vulgarity and indecency as was heard and seen there would disgust a more hardened person than I. The next place visited was a gambling hell where all games of chance were being played. Men excited with drink and dally were recklessly staking their last dollar on the turn of a card or the throw of a dice. Women were cajoling and coaxing the tipsy men to stake their money on various games; the pockets were shrewdly picked by the fallen women or the more sober of the crowd. We soon tired of this place and started forth for new dens of vice and crime and visited several similar to those already described. At last, about ten P.M. we visited the theater and were asked behind the curtains to see the girls. From here I left the party and retired to my tent fully satisfied with my first visit to such places."

Interestingly enough, Henry Morgan Stanley from the *St. Louis Missouri-Democrat* had a different take on Julesberg: "[I was] really astonished at the extraordinary growth of the town, and the energy of the people. It was unmistakable go-ahead-it-ative-ness, illustrated by substantial warehouses, stores, saloons, piled with goods of all sorts, and of the newest fashion. As might be expected, gambling was carried on extensively, and the saloons were full. I walked on till I came to a dance-house, bearing the euphonious title of 'King of the Hills,' gorgeously decorated and brilliantly lighted. Coming suddenly from the dimly lighted street to the kerosene-lighted restaurant, I was almost blinded by the glare and stunned by the clatter. The ground floor was as crowded as it could well be, and all were talking loud and fast, and mostly everyone seemed bent on debauchery, and dissipation. The women appeared to be the most reckless, and the men seemed nothing loth to enter a whirlpool of sin.... These women are expensive articles, and come in for a large share of the money wasted. In broad daylight they may be seen gliding through the sandy streets in Black Crook dresses, carrying fancy derringers slung to their waists, with which tools they are dangerously expert. Should they get into a fuss, western chivalry will not allow them to be abused by any man whom they may have robbed. At night new aspects are presented in this city of premature growth. Watch-fires gleam over the sea-like expanse of ground outside of the city, while inside soldiers, herdsmen, teamsters, women, railroad men, are dancing, singing, or gambling. I verily believe that there are men here who would murder a fellow-creature for five dollars. Nay, there are men who have already done it, and who stalk abroad in daylight unwhipped of justice. Not a day passes but a dead body is found somewhere in the vicinity with pockets rifled of their contents. But the people generally are strangely indifferent to what is going on."

Some of these towns remained so completely lawless that they soon evaporated, peppering the American West with its now famous ghost towns. However, as most towns grew, the number of citizens who wanted law and order came to outnumber those just looking for a good time, and as that happened, citizens began to organize themselves into "vigilance" groups whose members soon became known as vigilantes. For instance, in one burgeoning town, according to W.O. Owen, "It was the consensus of opinion that something had to be done. Accordingly, a vigilance committee was organized and its first act was the hanging of a boy known as 'The Kid.' This act of the vigilantes served only to intensify the bitter feeling of the lawless element and these now threatened openly to burn the town. … Early the following day my chum and I hastened to the Keane log building and viewed the bodies . . . We then returned to the streets and had been there only a short time when our attention was attracted to a body of men coming down the street. The party had in their midst a man known as 'Long Steve,' who was talking excitedly. He begged them to let him go. 'Boys,' he said, 'for God's sake let me go and I'll start right down that railroad track and never stop til I get to Omaha!' They then crossed the street to a telegraph pole, which stood near the Union Pacific Railway Company's oil house and executed the poor wretch in the presence of a large crowd. The hangings made Laramie about as safe a town to live in as could be found on the continent."

As this was going on elsewhere, the Central Pacific finally completed the infamous Summit Tunnel. According to Mark Hopkins, one of the workers, "It was a pleasant sight to reach such a point where a train would gravitate towards the East. For these years past gravitation has been so continually against us that at times it seemed to me that it would have been well if we had practiced a while on smaller and shorter hills before attacking so huge a mountain…. Our [Union Pacific] friends were too highly favored, but still we have worked up the mountain—the labored and rapid puff of the engine told how heavy and hard the work. At last we have reached the summit, are on the downgrade and we rejoice."

Put It On Their Line or Quit

A picture of the railroad near Cheyenne, Wyoming

The Devil's Gate Bridge in Utah

"If this is to be so, we better give up our road where it is and stop our work. I have no idea of doing this as Browning desires. He evidently wants to force us to give up our grading and take that of the Central and build our road on their line or lose our subsidy. The old hypocrite! I thought when he was saying to us that the location of this line in advance of ours gave them no rights he meant what he said, and would simply ask that the roads should be joined when they met. You must get some immediate action of Congress to have this matter put right and not let our line be sacrificed in this way. The idea that men like Browning are to sit in their office and fix the line on which these roads shall run when they have not seen or examined the line of our road nor know anything of it or either of them. I see no way for us to act if Browning's action is sustained but to withdraw our forces and wait for Central to build the road. We can't go on without the subsidy and if the subsidy is to be applied to their line we must pull up our track and put it on their line or quit." - Oliver Ames

Thrilled with its burst of progress, the Central Pacific was determined to make up for lost time.

In late 1867, Crocker wired Huntington, "If the Union Company lay more track '68 than we do I will pay the damage. We will beat the Union Pacific to Salt Lake. Stick a pin in there." His determination would be sorely tried, especially after he heard rumors that the Union Pacific was threatening, when they got close enough, to send an advance crew to Salt Lake "so as to preoccupy the ground and then take their time in building the road between." This was something Crocker was determined never to allow, writing, "Now I don't expect either they or we can gain anything by a trick. Congress I think would promptly put a stop to anything of that kind. But even if Congress did not intervene it would avail them nothing. We will, of course, go right on in good faith, grading a reasonable distance in advance to keep the tracklayers steady at work. If in so doing we should meet a company of Union Pacific graders, or a portion of road graded by them, not connected with a continuous line, we would keep right on, grade our road right alongside their grading until we should "meet & connect" with their continuous line of track, get our Commissioners to report on it, & draw our Govt. bonds in the usual way. They would throw away some money on grading (which however might perhaps be used when a double track should be necessary) & would feel rather cheap besides."

The early months of 1868 witnessed the Union Pacific reach the top of the Rocky Mountains, and from that point forward, it was a race to the end, with Huntington driving his partners and commanding them, "Make it cheap. When you can make any time in the construction by using wood instead of iron for culverts, etc., do it, and if we should now and then have a piece of the Road washed out for want of a culvert, we could put one in thereafter."

As more and more trains made their way east, the chances of an accident grew exponentially. With only telegraphs for communication, each train had to wait in a station until receiving the all clear to move on. Obviously, this slowed production, something that both companies found intolerable, and as such, they began taking more chances and losing more lives, not to mention time and materials.

As the Union Pacific got closer to Salt Lake, it was able to hire more workers from among the many Mormon settlers in the area. That last summer of 1869 proved to be the worst season yet for the project, as many men and animals died from heat and exertion in the desert. Meanwhile, the Central Pacific was picking up its pace, now laying down as much a six miles of track a day. When Casement heard about this, he managed to top that record by pushing his team to lay down seven miles of track in a single day.

Not only was work on the tracks hard, but the companies were now having to build structures to house their rolling stock and other supplies. On July 23, 1868, one correspondent wrote from Cheyenne, Dakota for *Harper's Weekly*, "On Monday last our party visited the car works and machine shops of the Union Pacific Railroad, at Omaha, and were not a little astonished at the magnitude of those works. ... As we entered the buildings the noise of twenty or thirty different machines all in motion -- the brawny workmen wielding ponderous sledge hammers -- the endless whirr of swift-revolving wheels -- the glowing metal, as it was taken at a white heat from the furnaces, scattering its bright sparks on every side -- all spoke of a busy, active life springing up here on these Western plains, where in our imagination we fancied we would see nothing but herds of buffalo and Indian encampments. ... There are men who would call the din and noise created by these various machines, all whizzing away in a confused harmony.... In the main building were several locomotives of immense power and fine finish, most of them having been manufactured at Trenton, N.J., but put together here in the shops of the Union Pacific Railroad, where all repairs are done also. The Company manufacture most of their own cars, both freight and passenger cars."

In 1869, an Eastern newspaper described the work on the railroad: "A light car, drawn by a single horse, gallops up to the front with its load of rails. Two men seize the end of a rail and start forward, the rest of the gang taking hold by twos, until it is clear of the car. They come forward at a run. At the word of command the rail is dropped in its place, right side up with care, while the same process goes on at the other side of the car. Less than thirty seconds to a rail for each gang, and so four rails go down to the minute ... close behind the first gang come the gaugers, spikers, and bolters, and a lively time they make of it. It is a grand 'anvil chorus' ... It is played in triple time, 3 strokes to the spike. There are 10 spikes to a rail, 400 rails to a mile, 1,800 miles to San Francisco — 21,000,000 times those sledges to be swung: 21,000,000 times are they to come down with their sharp punctuation before the great work of modern America is complete."

While the press was praising the work being completed, it was not so crazy about the way in which the construction was being financed, as it was becoming increasingly obvious that nearly everyone involved in governing the project was either taking or receiving illegal money and/or information. Eventually, the population began clamoring for justice, and on April 1, 1869, a little more than a month before the project's completion, the *New York Times* opined, "A great deal of Congressional wisdom has been wasted in pretended efforts to investigate the affairs of these railroads, but two or three days' work before a Court of justice has sufficed to lay bare one of the most monstrous frauds that was ever perpetrated upon any Government. ... We think it is about time that Congress should leave this matter alone.... Bad as may be our State Courts, there is no evidence or appearance in this case of any injustice having been done to these directors; and our Courts have done good service to the public in throwing light upon these transactions. The attempt to transfer the case to the Federal Courts is not inspired by a love of justice, but by a desire to protect gigantic frauds from exposure."

One of the Most Important Lines of Communication

Pictures of the Jupiter (the train that took Stanford to the Golden Spike ceremony)

"Across the Sierra Nevadas— The Central Pacific Railroad— the Western Half of the Great National Trunk Line Across the Continent, Being Constructed with the Aid and Supervision of the United States Government, is destined to be one of the most important lines of communication in the world, as it is the sole link between the Pacific Coast and the Great Interior Basin, over which the immense overland travel must pass, and the Principal Portion of the Main Stem Line between the two Oceans. Its line extends from Sacramento, on the tidal waters of the Pacific, eastward across the richest and most populous parts of California, Nevada and Utah, contiguous to all the great mining regions of the Far West, and will meet and connect with the roads now building east of the Rocky Mountains. About 100 miles are now built, equipped, and In running operation to the summit of the Sierra Nevada. Within a few days 35 miles, now graded, will be added, and the track carried entirely across the mountains to a point in the Great Salt Lake Valley, whence further progress will be easy and rapid. Iron, materials and equipment are ready at hand for 300 miles of road, and 10,000 men are employed in the construction." – A newspaper advertisement for the railroad

By January 1869, the end was in sight, and it was time for the representatives from each company to meet together and decide where the two tracks would come together. However, the men had been at each other's throats for so long that it was initially impossible for them to agree on anything. When Huntington, Oliver Ames and Dodge met in Washington, the meeting dissolved into a mutual shouting match, but since the crews had now passed each other and were actually laying track just 100 feet apart, it was critical that something be agreed upon. Finally, the men chose Promontory Summit, referred to by historian David Bain as "the most God-forsaken place that you could imagine."

As his final tribute to the project, Crocker pushed the crew of the Central Pacific to finish 10 miles of track in one day, a prodigious feat that set a new record (and one that still stands today). Author David Bain described the scene: "One by one, platform cars dumped their iron, two miles of material in each trainload, and teams of Irishmen fairly ran the five-hundred-pound rails and hardware forward. Straighteners led the Chinese gangs shoving the rails in place and keeping them to gauge while spikers walked down the ties, each man driving one particular spike and not stopping for another, moving on to the next rail; levelers and fillers followed, raising ties where needed, shoveling dirt beneath, tamping and moving on..." One man working on the project said to Crocker, "Mr. Crocker, I never saw such organization as that; it was like an army marching over the ground and leaving a track built behind them." When he heard about the record, Crocker's partner, Collis P. Huntington, responded ruefully, "It was an amazing thing. I wish they would have done it when it made a difference."

On May 10, 1869, the entire country seemed to hold its breath as, under the brightest of blue skies, the men prepared to lay the final track. As the whole nation awaited the completion, the telegraphers prepared for the last hit:

> "Omaha Telegraph: 'To everybody: keep quiet. When the last spike is driven ... we will say 'done.' Don't break the circuit, but watch for the blows of the hammer.'
>
> Promontory Telegraph: 'Almost ready. Hats off. Prayer is being offered.'
>
> Chicago Telegraph: 'We understand. All are ready in the east.'
>
> Promontory Telegraph: 'All ready now. The spike will soon be driven. The signal will be three dots for the commencement of the blow.'"

Alexander Toponce was there that day and described the Golden Spike ceremony that marked the completion of the project:

> "On the last day, only about 100 feet were laid, and everybody tried to have a hand in the work. I took a shovel from an Irishman, and threw a shovel full of dirt on the ties just to tell about it afterward. A special train from the west brought…a lot of newspaper men, and plenty of the best brands of champagne.

Another train made up at Ogden carried the band from Fort Douglas, the leading men of Utah Territory, and a small but efficient supply of Valley Tan. California furnished the Golden Spike. Governor Tuttle of Nevada furnished one of silver. General Stanford presented one of gold, silver, and iron from Arizona. The last tie was of California laurel.

When they came to drive the last spike, Governor Stanford, president of the Central Pacific, took the sledge, and the first time he struck he missed the spike and hit the rail. What a howl went up! ... Then Stanford tried it again and tapped the spike and the telegraph operators had fixed their instruments so that the tap was reported in all the offices east and west, and set bells to tapping in hundreds of towns and cities.... Then Vice President T. C. Durant of the Union Pacific took up the sledge and he missed the spike the first time. Then everybody slapped everybody else again and yelled, 'He missed it too, yow!' ... When the connection was finally made the Union Pacific and the Central Pacific engineers ran their engines up until their pilots touched. Then the engineers shook hands and had their pictures taken and each broke a bottle of champagne on the pilot of the other's engine and had their picture taken again."

Thomas Hill's painting of the completion of the railroad

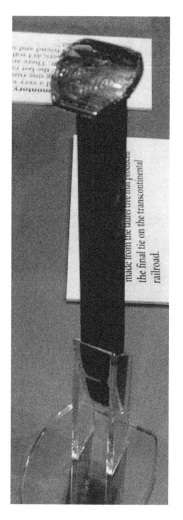

Quatro Valvole's picture of 1 of the 4 Golden Spikes used at the ceremony

Of course, that day in May marked not an end but a beginning. For both railroad companies, it was the beginning of maintaining and improving tracks that they soon wished they had more time to build right in the first place. For those on the East Coast, it meant a chance to safely make their way to new homes and new lives out west. Wives would be able to join their husbands, and children could rejoin their fathers. Likewise, the many unmarried women despairing of finding husbands out east after the Civil War could go west and find families or at least careers teaching school. For those already living on the West Coast, there would be many new opportunities to bring in supplies and visit family members in far off Kansas.

An advertisement for the railroad

Unfortunately, the future was not bright for everyone. The scandals and graft surrounding the building of the railroad would prove to be a thorn in the side of many politicians for the next several years, reaching all the way to White House and President Ulysses Grant. Nonetheless, looking back on it all in 1869 and commenting on the railroad's incredible importance, Albert Richardson observed:

> "The Atlantic is nearer to the Pacific than New York was to Boston fifty years ago. Going to California by our luxurious eating, sleeping, and drawing-room cars, is a wonder and a delight as contrasted with the old plains and mountain, or ocean and isthmus travel. At noon in New York it is nine A. M. in San

Francisco. The line is so long that trains upon it are run by eight or ten different times. Ultimately we shall have a double set of hands upon all watches—one for local time, and one for general time—uniform all over the world. ... Some sanguine writers believe that by running steamers and locomotives at their utmost speed, the entire time can be reduced to three weeks—ten days from Yokohama to San Francisco, four from there to New York, and seven from New York to London; but for the present we may be abundantly satisfied with nearly twice that time. Upon these closing lines my pen lingers, and I listen for the voice of the future brakeman. Day after day, on the continental journey, he opens his door and shouts to sleepy passengers:

'Chicago. Change cars for New Orleans and Lake Superior.'

'Missouri River. Change cars for Saskatchewan, Kansas City, and Galveston.'

...'San Francisco. Passengers for New Zealand, Honolulu, Melbourne, Yokohama, Hong Kong, and all other points in Asia, Africa, and Europe will keep their seats till landed on the wharf of the daily line of the Pacific Mail Steamship Company. Baggage checked through to Pekin, Calcutta, Grand Cairo, Constantinople, St. Petersburg, Paris, and Liverpool!'"

The Panama Canal

The Origins of the Canal

"The United States has taken the position that no other government is to build the canal." – President Theodore Roosevelt

Although the completion of the Panama Canal in the 1910s was the culmination of over a decade of work carried out mostly by the United States, Americans were hardly the first people to think of building a canal to connect the two oceans. In fact, explorers and sailors had been talking about it for centuries, ever since someone realized that there was only one tiny strip of land preventing them from have to sail around the coast of South America to reach the Pacific Ocean. Indeed, the Americans were not the first to try to build such a canal; the French began trying to create a waterway across the Isthmus of Panama in 1880, bringing in Ferdinand de Lesseps, who had famously dug the Suez Canal, to head up the project.

Ferdinand de Lesseps

However, the terrain across which the French had built the Suez Canal was completely different from that in Panama, and they were ultimately unsuccessful. After eight years of blood, sweat and tears, including the loss of 20,000 lives, the project was bankrupt and the idea of constructing any sort of canal across Panama was seen as a hopeless cause.

Pictures of French work on the canal in the 19th century

Then came Theodore Roosevelt, who succeeded William McKinley to the presidency in 1901. An avid outdoorsman who had spent time ranching and had fought in Cuba with the Rough Riders, Roosevelt was the kind of man willing to pursue causes that would test the physical limits of men. If America needed a canal in Panama, Roosevelt would be the type of man willing to make the attempt. On January 4, 1904, he announced to Congress, "The United States has taken the position that no other government is to build the canal. In 1889, when France proposed to come to the aid of the French Panama Company by guaranteeing their bonds, the Senate of the United States in Executive session, with only some three votes dissenting, passed a resolution as follows: 'That the Government of the United States will look with serious concern and disapproval upon any connection of any European government with the construction or control of any ship canal across the Isthmus of Darien or across Central America…' Under the Hay-Pauncefote treaty it was explicitly provided that the United States should control, police, and protect the canal which was to be built, keeping it open for the vessels of all nations on equal terms. The United States thus assumed the position of guarantor of the canal and of its peaceful use by all the world. The guarantee included as a matter of course the building of the canal. The enterprise was recognized as responding to an international need; and it would be the veriest travesty on right and justice to treat the governments in possession of the Isthmus as having the right, in the language of Mr. Cass, 'to close the gates of intercourse on the great highways of the world, and justify the act by the pretension that these avenues of trade and travel belong to them and that they choose to shut them.'"

Roosevelt

1896 picture of the Culebra cut

A 1902 picture of the Culebra cut

Roosevelt mentioned the Europeans, but in addition to the physical difficulty, there was another major obstacle: the land across which the United States wanted to build the canal was owned by Colombia, a sovereign country. In fact, the Columbian constitution forbade its leaders from yielding any sovereignty to an outside interest, so they refused to allow America to build and control a canal in their country. Roosevelt complained about this: "In our anxiety to be fair we had gone to the very verge in yielding to a weak nation's demands what that nation was helplessly unable to enforce from us against our will. The only criticisms made upon the Administration…were for having granted too much to Colombia, not for failure to grant enough. Neither in the Congress nor in the public press…was there complaint that it did not in the fullest and amplest manner guarantee to Colombia everything that she could by any color of title demand. Nor is the fact to be lost sight of that…while generously responding to the pecuniary demands of Colombia, in other respects merely provided for the construction of the canal in conformity with the express requirements of the act of the Congress of June 28, 1902. By that act, as heretofore quoted, the President was authorized to acquire from Colombia, for the purposes of the canal, 'perpetual control' of a certain strip of land; and it was expressly required that the 'control' thus to be obtained should include 'jurisdiction' to make police and sanitary regulations and to establish such judicial tribunals as might be agreed on for their enforcement."

Many colonial powers might have just gone in and taken the area by force, and such a move might not have been surprising coming from a man who coined the phrase "speak softly and carry a big stick," but Roosevelt soon came a across another option. He learned that a group of Panamanian leaders had been wanting to secede from Columbia for years, but they simply didn't have the manpower to accomplish it. Thus, Roosevelt aided them by sending an American gunboat to Colon to offer the rebels support when they revolted on November 3, 1903. As revolutions go, it was a pretty tame one, and it was over by the end of the day with only one casualty. Of course, part of the reason that the revolution was so tame was that the United States had paid most of the Columbian soldiers not to fight. Three days later, the United States became the first nation to recognize the newly formed country of Panama, and in gratitude, the newly chosen Panamanian leaders gave America a 500 mile section of land on which to build a canal.

We Can Do That

"So, Goethals and old big wheel, they got together and said, okay, we can do that. We can build that canal, but how are you going to do it? …we'll get some engineers that will do it for us. … These engineers from the Corps of Engineers, Goethals, and all those guys, they looked the area over. … You go over and you look it all over and say, well, this is all you have to do to this. …we can move a hill. … You take a bucket and put some sand in it. Take it over here and dump it. Then you're going to take a pail and fill it up full of sand and you're going to take it way over here. Oh, well we're going to build a little railroad on that land. Okay, we'll build a little railroad and take it over here half a mile and we'll just keep doing that and maybe in four or five years we'll have it done. Well ten years later they had it done. They got up in the hills, they got some dynamite; we're going to blast that. So they blast it. These big hills. Bucyrus-Erie…Lorain was another one: great big steam shovels. They could probably pick up four or five ton at a time. So they built a little railroad." - Leo Krziza, grandson of a canal worker

America's first step in building the canal took place on May 4, 1904, but while John Findley Wallace was nominally in charge of the project, he soon learned that he was not really in charge.

Instead, ultimate power rested with the Isthmian Canal Commission, a group of men handpicked by Roosevelt to build the canal. Among their strictest orders from the president was that they were not to waste a single dime of taxpayer money, which led to a backlog of requests for materials and supplies that nearly derailed the entire project.

John Fishley Wallace

Wallace

Another problem facing Wallace was that there was no definitive plan for how the canal should be constructed. Instead, he was told to start where the French had started and continue the work they had left behind, beginning in Colon on the east coast of the isthmus and going to Panama City on the west coast. This would eventually take the canal through some of the densest jungle in South America, as well as through a narrow valley in the Culebra Mountains, a situation that concerned Wallace from the beginning. With only 3,500 men to accomplish this feat, he pleaded for more time, at least a year, to get to know the terrain and the equipment at his disposal. Undeterred by the challenges, Roosevelt would not grant his wishes, so Wallace had to go ahead and "make the dirt fly."

19th century excavation work in the Culebra mountains

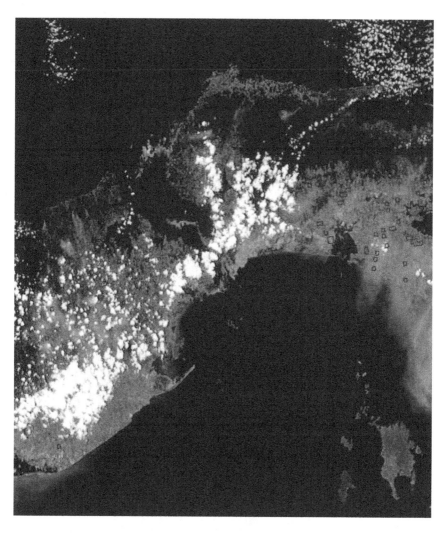

A satellite image of the location of the Panama Canal

Thus, in November 1904, Wallace began his first tentative efforts to cut through the Culebra. He had for this purpose two 95-ton steam shovels that were capable of moving eight tons of earth with every scoop. Of course, moving the earth was one thing, but getting rid of it was another, and for that, he needed railroad cars, something he never seemed to have enough of. He could "make the dirt fly" all he wanted, but without trains to take it away, it just fell back to the ground, halting the process. John Stevens, who later replaced Wallace, criticized the initial plans: "Doubtless the old commission, in deference to the idiotic howl about 'making the dirt fly,' had instructed Mr. Wallace to try and do so with the means at hand (for I am convinced that, of his own volition, would have done no such thing), which meant with the exception of a few modern steam shovels, he had to resurrect a lot old, small, and decrepit French plant, and hammer away as best he could. Engines, cars and track were all pitifully ludicrous, and no progress worth the name could be made. Standing on one point, overlooking a part of Culebra Cut, a short time after my arrival, I counted seven work trains in the ditch, and all visible shovels idle. And all available forces of laborers were trying to get these trains on to the tracks, an unwise proceeding, for they were of more value where they were."

Stevens

Then there was the matter of living conditions. Jan van Hardeveld, who came to the Canal Zone from Wyoming, wrote to his family, "The food is awful, and cooked in such a way that no civilized white man can stand it for more than a week or two. These native women have nothing to cook on but little iron charcoal braziers just large enough to hold one pot at a time. Almost all the food is fried. They feed us fried green bananas, boiled rice, and foul-smelling salt fish. It rains so much that honest to goodness my hat is getting moldy on my head. I'm convinced there isn't a place in the world that can beat the Isthmus for rain. Every day and every night it pours down. I haven't had on a pair of dry shoes in weeks. More water falls from the skies here in six days than does in six years in Wyoming. ... I grew careless last week, and before I realized it, I was one sick hombre -- stomach out of order, and my blood full of malaria bugs. Now I live with a bottle of liquid quinine in one pocket and a bottle of Epsom salts solution in the other. I'm taking no more chances that I can help of being sent home wrapped in a wooden overcoat, although they tell me the Government dresses each American in a metallic one, when it becomes necessary to send him home in that style."

At first, it seemed that the canal might indeed be impossible to build, and the workers were no doubt fully aware that they were surrounded day and night by the remnants of past failures. Within just a few months, 500 Americans who had travelled down to the canal to work had returned to the United States. One man wrote to his mother, "I am thoroughly sick of this country and everything to do with the canal. Tell the boys at home to stay there, even if they get no more than a dollar a day."

A Loyal American Citizen

"My connection with the Panama Canal began on July, 1, 1905, my appointment as chief engineer of the Isthmian Canal Commission taking effect upon that date, to succeed Mr. John F. Wallace, who had resigned three days previously. ...as the matter was presented to me, in view of the discouraging condition into which affairs had drifted during the period of American occupation, as a loyal American citizen, and as a cordial supporter of an administration which was represented as being much exercised over the situation, it became my duty to waive personal inclinations, and to accept the responsibilities of the position. I accordingly did so, and the arrangement verbally agreed upon ... was confirmed by the chairman of the commission, on the date noted." - John Stevens, Chief Engineer

Although men were dropping out by the hundreds, there were others who seemed compelled to continue by an audacious patriotism that made them believe anything was possible. Van Hardeveld explained this sentiment: "The slowness of the work would be discouraging, if I were not certain that our Government can and will accomplish whatever it sets out to do. You know what I always say -- in America, anything is possible ... That is why, since you have made no objection, I have made my decision to stay -- and I am happy to be able to tell you that the quartermaster has at last assigned me to married quarters. The house is an old one at Las Cascadas, the village near where I am now working. It was the first house build here by the French, and it is marked 'House Number One.' This will be our chance to be among those who make history! Your Papa is helping to build the big canal, the waterway that has been in the minds of men for centuries. This canal, when it is finished, will change the face of the earth. It will unite the two oceans, the Atlantic and the Pacific, and alter the course of the ships that sail upon them. Yes, children, we will be among those who make history!"

Unfortunately, Wallace did not shared his men's optimism and soon became overwhelmed by his task. He ultimately resigned in June 1905, and at that point, the United States had already invested $78 million in the project only to have almost no progress. Desperate to make the project work, Roosevelt appointed John Stevens, a man best known for his work on the Great Northern Railroad, to replace Wallace. For his part, Stevens saw the canal commission, called the Walker Commission after its chairman, as the source of most of the problems. He later wrote, "I sailed for the Canal Zone, landing there on July 26, taking immediate and personal charge of all affairs there (excepting government and sanitation), including the Panama Railroad, and I believe I faced about as discouraging a proposition as was ever presented to a construction engineer. ... The ineffective organization of the Walker commission, the utter lack of responsibility definitely located, the endeavor to decide and act upon the most trivial matters, at a distance of two thousand miles by a body of seven men, each of equal rank, who were apparently unable to agree with each other, or with anybody else, would have been sufficient reason for a partial, or even a total failure, no matter who might have been the chief engineer."

Thankfully, Stevens had the self-confidence and determination that Wallace lacked, and he immediately set to work to correct the deficiencies he observed. "With the light of what I could plainly see had been the experience of Mr. Wallace, I determined from the start, or as soon as I could grasp the significance of affairs, that the only line of policy that promised success was one of going ahead and doing things on my own initiative, without waiting for orders or approval. One of the terms I insisted upon before I became chief engineer was that I should be unhampered in my work in any way, shape or manner, and I am free to say this agreement was strictly kept. The distance of the commission from the work as well as its make-up, did not admit of any other plan of procedure. As constituted, the members of the commission, who were civil engineers, were designated to act in an advisory capacity. But I knew full well that none of the board had the experience in either such construction work or transportation matters that would qualify them to dictate to me how matters should be planned and handled, and frankly I determined early that they should not."

The first step Stevens took was the most dramatic: ordering all work to stop until he could get a firm grasp on the situation. To do this, he first turn his attention to the Panama Railroad. He noted, "The reconstruction of the Panama Railroad, which was under my management, was a serious problem. It was not, at the time I took charge, able to handle its commercial business, with the additional traffic already thrown onto it, and a very serious state of congestion prevailed. Owing to the delay in deciding upon the type of the canal, it was not possible to rebuild it upon a permanent location; at the same time, the extraordinary amount and variety of service it was called upon to render made quick decision and vigorous action necessary. ... Plans were made, the work of reconstruction pushed, -- hampered all the while by the necessity of handling the constantly increasing traffic -- until in 1906 the railroad had been practically rebuilt, double-tracked, supplied with all necessary accessories, including those demanded by food and other supply reception and distribution, and was fully capable of, and did handle satisfactorily, every burden put upon it."

Stevens' move was a wise one, as the railroad was necessary not just for hauling dirt but also for bringing in fresh workers and a constant stream of supplies. That said, equipping them to be more efficient in moving dirt proved to be his most important feat. Using his own experience and working with some of the best minds in the area, he had a series of open-sided flat cars built, each with a plow on it that could empty the dirt pile on it in minutes. He also designed the tracks so they could be easily moved to a new area of work when necessary, and he made sure that, whenever possible, the cars went uphill empty and downhill full, taking much of the strain of hauling tons of material uphill off of the engines.

Even with that logistical issue solved, the most intimidating challenge of the project still lay ahead of the men: cutting the canal through Culebra. Of this, Stevens wrote, "We must reflect that at best, even with the backing and sentiment and finances of the most powerful nation on earth, that we are contending with Nature's forces, and that while our wishes and ambition are for great assistance in a work of this magnitude, neither the inspiration of genius nor our optimism will build this canal. Nothing but dogged determination and steady, persistent, intelligent work will ever accomplish the result; and when we speak of a hundred million years of a sing cut not to excess nine miles in length, we are facing a proposition greater than was ever undertaken in the engineering history of the world."

38-A- Culebra Cut Looking North – Dec., 1904.

A 1904 picture of work on the Culebra cut

A 1907 picture of work in the Gaillard cut

Stevens' problems were well known among those living in the area, one of whom wrote, "I heard much about the dissatisfaction of the men. They all complained about the labor; it was impossible to teach these blacks or to trust them. The second chief engineer, Mr. Stevens, was doing a fine job reorganizing, but he was having his troubles. No one knew whether the canal was to be a sea-level or a lock canal. Colonel William Gorgas was having difficulty in getting enough material for the adequate sanitary program, which was of such importance. About a mile to the south we could see Empire. Culebra lay a half mile beyond that. At both of these towns a number of American families had already arrived, and schools were being established for the children."

Then there was the problem of the Chagres River, which swelled with water to the point of overflowing during the rainy season of 1905 and stopped all work for at least six months. If the project had to work around the river, the project could be delayed by as much as a decade. It was at this point that Stevens made his most important decision yet by determining that the canal could not be built at sea level, as the French had attempted to do. Instead, the canal would have to be constructed in such a way that ships could get through it by traveling over the mountains. To explain this seemingly impossible plan, Stevens traveled to Washington to meet with Roosevelt in person. He later confided, "The time devoted to the discussion of the type of the proposed canal, both on the Isthmus and in Washington, seemed endless, but the part I took in it, which, without conceit, I think had some influence in the decision made, will ever be a source of gratification to me personally. I went to the Isthmus with a fairly open mind on the subject of type -- if anything, rather inclined in favor of the sea level. But it did not take me long to realize that however rich and powerful in men and resources the United States might be, the idea of a sea-level canal, such as proposed, was absurd; that a practical one could not be built in any admissible length of time, or without the expenditure of a totally unjustifiable amount of money -- enough to stagger even the financial ability of the nation. So I became an earnest advocate of the present completed lock-type, and reported to the commission strongly in its favor, and both before the International Board of engineers and committees of both House and Senate, and with individual members of these bodies, earnestly urged its merits; and felt then, and do yet, that the decision which was made in its favor was eminently wise, and that time will so fully demonstrate. Visits to the States, solely on canal affairs, took up much valuable time which I felt could much better have been devoted to affairs on the Isthmus, but they seemed to be considered necessary, and were made, although several times under protest."

The type of canal that Stevens was proposing was amazing in its scale but not in its concept; indeed, it was actually based on previous efforts in other parts of the world. In essence, Stevens was planning to dam up the Chagres River at Gatun and thus create a manmade lake located 85 feet above sea level. Thus, when a ship entered the canal, it would pass through a series of locks that would raise it to the height of the lake, after which the ship would sail across the lake and be lowered by another series of locks on the other side. Each of these locks was a huge concrete pool (larger than three football fields) that could be filled and emptied by opening and closing various dams at either end. As Stevens wrote to Roosevelt, "There is no element of mystery involved in it. The problem is one of magnitude, not miracles."

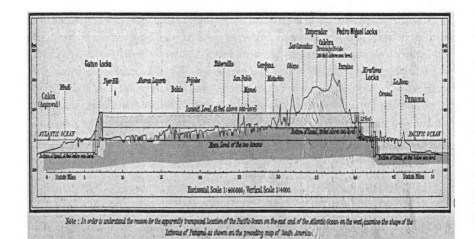

Note : In order to understand the reason for the apparently transposed location of the Pacific Ocean on the east and of the Atlantic Ocean on the west, examine the shape of the Isthmus of Panamá as shown on the preceding map of South America.

A diagram of the different water levels of the Panama Canal

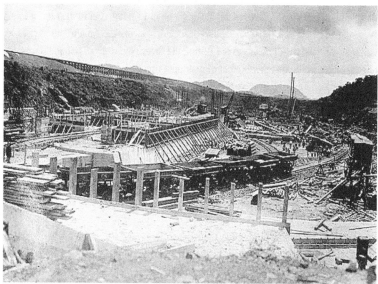

Pictures of a lock under construction

The Apartheid System

"The apartheid system governed every aspect of a worker's life. The distinction began as a division between 'skilled' and 'unskilled' laborers, but as time passed it evolved into a purely racial divide. Skilled employees went on the Gold Roll and were paid in gold coins. These workers earned paid sick and vacation time and were housed in better accommodations than their unskilled counterparts. Those on the Silver Roll, the unskilled workers, were paid in balboas, or local Panamanian silver. West Indian workers, plentiful in numbers and eager to work, could be paid 10 cents an hour -- half of the salary of a European or white U.S. worker. Over time, the Gold Roll became comprised of white U.S. citizens exclusively, while the workers on the Silver Roll, by far the majority of the workforce by the end of the construction period, were largely non-white." – An anonymous author writing about working on the canal

Part of the problem that many workers and their families faced was a form of culture shock, for America at that time was a highly segregated society. In fact, anyone who had never traveled to a large city or into the southern United States might never have seen a non-white person. However, most of the workers who had been brought in to work on the canal came from the West Indian islands.

When she landed with her two daughters in Panama, Rose van Hardeveld got her first taste of what it meant to be a cultural and racial minority within a community. She explained, "A fine drizzly rain was falling. Black men, women, and children were going to and fro on the track, jabbering and gesticulating as they walked. A white man -- the only white person I had seen -- came along and held an umbrella over our heads. 'You must not go out in the rain,' he said. 'It will give you fever.' He was the local sanitary inspector. During the walk to our steps, I learned from him that we must by all means avoid getting the fever. We were so hot and uncomfortable by the time we got inside that the thought of making a fire in the pocket size cookstove was almost unbearable. The children were already broken out with prickly heat, and I felt as though I were being smothered between wet, evil-smelling sponges. I thanked my friendly neighbor, and prepared for another tramp in the heat. Passing by her house, I had to smother a gasp of dismay as I glanced at her and her small, almost naked boys. She talked like an American, and I knew she must be American, but her skin was yellow and taut. The little boys' teeth protruded from their pale lips, their abdomens were painfully distended, their knees knobby. Oh dear, I thought, as I looked at my round-cheeked rosy babies. I wonder how long it will be until we look like that?"

While she might not have thought of it, the workers Rose saw were actually experiencing a more severe culture shock than she was, because they too had been brought from their homes to work in a strange world. However, while she was white and therefore at the top of the sociopolitical food chain, they were of African descent and thus relegated to the bottom. John Stevens needed thousands of workers to build the canal, most of them unskilled, and to fill these positions, he brought in 15,000 men from the West Indies. The plan was that they would dig ditches and cut brush while the 5,000 white Americans took easier and better paying jobs as skilled laborers, thus working as carpenters, blacksmiths, plumbers, and the like. Egbert C. Leslie, one of the black men brought in as a canal worker, later wrote, "I landed here on the 21st of January, 1907. On the appearance of the place I felt like I'll go right back home because everything looked so strange and there no different to being brought up at home so I felt like I'd go back home, but it wasn't so easy to do that."

In addition to the strange sights they saw, Rose and the others had to become accustomed to the sound of the trains that ran day and night, moving rock and earth out and people and supplies in. With a perspective typical of the time, she later wrote, "Trains had been rattling down the tracks all day but I paid no attention to them, until I heard a strange squeaky whistle. I reached the porch in time to see a most peculiar train pulling in from the north. The funny, old-fashioned engine halted right at our board-walk. There were a dozen cars, of the cattle car type, filled to overflowing with black men. Before the train stopped, they were dropping off and spreading out like a colony of black ants."

The men she saw traveling in such conditions that day had come from a great distance for the promise of good pay. In reality, they were young and had fallen prey to some one of the best advertising campaigns of the 20th century. Marco Mason, whose grandfather was among them, explained, "They created what was called the Panama Man, which was to get someone that went to Panama and bring him back and he will be the advertiser. And what he came back -- when he came back to Barbados from Panama, he came back with white trousers, white jacket, gold teeth, Panama hat, a big smile and monies in their pocket. And all the other guys in the plantation take a look and say, 'boy I better go down to Panama and get mine too.'" Of course, once these workers arrived, they found reality much different. "They had shacks and they had bunk beds on all four walls. All four walls had bunk beds, three layers of bunk beds. Very harsh facilities. That was part and parcel of that type of society that was created."

John W. Bowen was one of the men who believed in the promises made by "the Panama Man." He recalled, "I had some friends and they always getting ready to go and they wanted me to go, and I joined them and I left from St. Lucy. Went to Bridgetown to the transportation office and I signed up there for a trip to the Canal. I had no recognition of what was going to happen. I couldn't conceive. I hadn't yet seen the canal. I hadn't yet seen no part of the operation until after I reached employment then I began to realize what a stupendous affair this would be."

Part of the culture shock came from the determined, driven way in which Americans work. The people of the islands, accustomed to the incredibly hot and draining weather, knew better than to work too hard in the middle of the day, and they had lifestyles more in keeping with a warm climate where work could be done at any time of the year. The Americans, on the other hand, were primarily from cooler areas and were thus inclined to work at the frenzied pace they had developed in a world where the growing season was short and the winter long. As a result, Americans often saw the islanders as lazy, while those from the islands saw them as irrational.

Spanish laborers working on the canal in the 1900s

Before long, the Canal Zone developed its own unique form of racism, one based on the currency in which one was paid. The skilled white workers were paid in gold, while the unskilled black workers were paid in silver. Therefore, throughout the region, signs went up designating which places were for "gold" workers and which belonged to those earning "silver." As William Daniel Donadio, the son of a canal worker, put it, "I remember my stepfather talking about it. It was a kind of a polished-up segregation. It didn't say black and white, but you understood that if you weren't a gold roller and you were a silver roller that you were on the black side."

To Make a Home

"I think the order of events was that the men were recruited and hired, in the United States. For instance, my grandfather in New York State was what you'd call a jack of all trades, master of none. ... So they hired these sorts of men, craftsmen, to come down and work. They took the men down on ships from New York, and after they got the men settled, the families were brought down. So, I always imagined a woman and her two small children. I think my mother was two years old, her brother was older, a little bit. Anyway, a woman who had never been outside the United States, goes down the New York City from Saratoga, New York, and gets on a ship with two small children to sail over the ocean to go somewhere strange. ... There was no air conditioning, a lot of people on board, and then they arrive in this place that's got a lot of mosquitoes and it rains a lot and it's hotter than blue blazes. They got to make a home there and they can't just turn around and take an airplane out of there." - Gerold Cooper, grandson of a canal builder

With a firm plan for the canal's future in place, van Hardeveld and many other workers felt secure enough in their future to bring their families to the area. However, for the women and children, many of whom would make their permanent homes there, the Canal Zone looked nothing like the paradise it would later become. Rose van Hardeveld, who joined her husband Jan in 1907, remembered, "As the train rolled out of the station, we soon saw where the smells came from. Houses were built on timbers right in the ocean. Green scummy water lashed and licked at the posts. Coconuts and rotten vegetables floated on the surface of the water. Naked brown children with tousled heads, and mangy-looking dogs stared listlessly at the train from the dismal vantage points along the track. It was a relief when the town was left behind and we plunged into the green jungle. A penetrating stench, so vile it was almost unbearable, had struck me the instant the door had opened for our entrance. "The bats. These French houses have stood unoccupied for years. They have double walls, and the space between the inner and outer walls is occupied by hundreds of bats. ... As if to comfort me with the knowledge that our situation was by no means the worst on the Isthmus, Jan described to me at some length how unsatisfactory conditions were everywhere on the canal. The big cry was 'Make the dirt fly!' -- but things had not yet reached the stage where the dirt could be made to fly. ... Dingy, nondescript houses sprawled up and down the hillsides. It did not have the appearance of a village that had been planned. It looked as though the people had become tired, dropped just about anywhere, and put up a shack on whatever spot they happened to be resting. There was not a street or a sidewalk. Instead of roads there were narrow footpaths worn by feet that walked from place to place on the rocky hillsides."

Picture of a steam shovel moving dirt

The Panama Canal Zone in 1907 was wilder than any American western town had ever been, a place where there were more than 100 single men for every female inhabitant. Far from home, they worked hard and they played hard, taking advantage of the many forms of entertainment that always spring up in such situations. Nobel Philips later relayed a story handed down in his family: "When my father got to Panama, he was broke and he had a relative or cousin or something like that that he knew was in Panama. … So, when he got to the old wooden bachelor quarters, he asked somebody, do you know so and so? And he says, oh yeah, he's upstairs running the poker game. … He said he went up there and introduced himself to his cousin or whatever it was, and the cousin was running the poker game and in front of him he had all gold coins. They were all paid in gold at that time. And my father told him he was broke and he lost his money playing poker on the way down. The fella says, that'll teach ya not to play poker, and never gave him a cent. So he had to get his money, 'til payday, from others that would help him out."

From a woman's perspective, the situation was shocking. Rose explained, "Between thirty and forty thousand alien people were to be brought into this area; the housing problem alone would be staggering. Colonel William Gorgas, the man who had done such outstanding work in Cuba with his fight against yellow fever, was on the Isthmian Canal Commission as chief health officer. Sanitation was of primary importance. Conditions were appalling in the cities of Colon and Panama, with their crooked gambling houses, filthy saloons and brothels. The well-known 'American sucker' had come to the Isthmus and was being properly fleeced by those who knew how. The authorities realized that the only way to counteract these evils was to bring to Panama the wives and children building of the canal. … In going to and fro between the shops I noticed dingy places bearing across the front the word Cantina. I did not know the meaning of the word, but by the smells around the places and the condition of the men and women coming out of them, I knew they must be saloons. It worried me to see little black children running in and out, freely, to see black women staggering, laughing, cursing, and to watch our own men going in for drinks. … I was told that the men needed some stimulant to cope with the climate, but I did not believe it. It seemed strange to me that alcohol could be such a general panacea, a warming agent in cold countries, a cooling agent in warm ones."

For the women who joined their husbands, moral concerns were not the most pressing needs; after all, they could avoid parts of town that offended their Edwardian sensibilities. However, food for their families was another matter and a constant source of concern, as Rose detailed: "We entered a whitewashed barn we suspected might be a store. A bald-pated Chinese in a cotton undershirt and loose white pantaloons shuffled toward us with a friendly grin, his bare feet thrust into straw sandals. I looked around, wondering if this could be a grocery store. Not one edible thing looked familiar, except five or six doubtful looking eggs, loose on the shelf. On the counter there was a pile of something that looked like long, angular green bananas. From the grocery store we went to the meat market, a sorry looking place indeed! About the size of a small clothes closet, but tightly screened, the place was almost hidden by flies. Ribbons of bloody beef hung suspended from nails around the walls. A rusty saw, hand-axe and knife lay on a shelf besides hunks of meat which had evidently been hacked from the same carcass that had furnished the ribbons of beef. The dark-skinned, bare-footed man inside looked hopefully at me as I approached, but it all looked so unappetizing that I turned away down the track to our house. … 'A government commissary will be in operation in a few days,' Jan said, 'at Empire, and we'll be able to have staples and canned milk from New York.'… I struggled bravely with my housekeeping problems throughout the afternoon. What furniture there was, was hopelessly old and shabby. The heat was too intense to venture forth again in search of food. The evil stench inside the house drove us at last out onto the porch, where we sat limply awaiting Jan's return."

Then there was the matter of setting up housekeeping in an environment so completely different from the one she was accustomed to: "The house had two rooms and an alcove. We put up the two beds. The mattresses were new, for which I was very thankful. We hung mosquito nets over the beds, for the house was not screened. … There was little furniture and little space in which to put it. A very small bedroom with an alcove, a smaller living room, and a tiny kitchen partitioned off one end of the screened veranda – this we were to call home. A long flight of wooden steps led from the front door and another from the kitchen door. A small building in the rear contained a shower room and a toilet. … Below us lay pieces of machinery overturned, strings of cars, engines, and twisted rails, all covered with growing vines and brush. Large trees had grown up through the couplings of a string of cars at the foot of the hill. The whole array told mutely of the hard-earned, penuriously saved money that had gone to purchase the equipment now lying there useless. 'A graveyard of a nation's dead hopes,' the Americans said. Some of the equipment was used for a while by the Isthmian Canal Commission, but it was too small and inadequate, and was finally sold to a Chicago wrecking company."

At the same time, living in Panama had its attractions, the primary one being the view of the jungle that had not yet been despoiled by the project. For all her complaining and disappointment, Rose was able to appreciate the surroundings and describe them: "The house was dingy behind description, but there was a wonderful view in every direction, since the building was raised from the ground on wooden posts. To the south lay the village, beyond that Empire, Culebra, Miraflores, Corozal, Ancon, Panama, and finally the Pacific Ocean. To the north, along the line of the track winding among the low hills, was Matachin, a small nondescript village; then Haut Obispo, no bigger or better; and then Bas Obispo. The good old Star Spangled Banner, doubly beautiful and precious in this strange country, flew from a pole on the top of a hill in Camp Elliott, the United States Marine Corps station at Bas Obispo. To the west, a panorama of palm-crowned hills rolled along at the edge of the horizon, their jungle-covered slopes bearing down to the very edge of the railroad track. Looking eastward from the back door, I got my first sight of the Canal. ... This was [the girls'] first real glimpse of the vast project, too enormous for their young minds to grasp, which was the whole purpose of our lives here in the strange, always uncomfortable and often frightening tropics."

Others found this to be true, including Nobel Philips' mother. He later said, "My mother went down ... into Colón. The house they had was over the water in Colón. It was on stilts and you had little walkways to go out to the houses—shacks—that were built over the water. She stayed there for about four or five months before they moved the machine shop. He worked at night times in the machine shop along Gatún there. Then, they moved to Culebra and that's when she was able to get a house. They had a house and they each had a small horse of the same kind. Kept it in the yard. ... There was a platform in a tree and steps, a ladder like, leading up to it. They would go up there with their long dresses and climb this place, into the tree, so that they could see the Pacific and the Atlantic at the same time. They were high enough to see both."

Back to Work on the Canal

"We took it from the French, we spent two years with Dr. Gorgas clearing the mosquitos out from 1904 to 1906. The mosquitos were cleaned out, that was done by filling in all the water places. There's actually evidence that at the Gorgas-Ancón Hospital, I guess it was called at that time, people were getting sick. So people in the hospital said, let's put the legs of the beds in tins of water, and that will keep all these insects from crawling up in the bed because they can't swim. Well those tins of water were breeding the mosquitos that were attacking the people. So they got that out, but by that time, the canal was fairly well cleaned up and they went back to work on the canal." - Malcom Stone, descendant of a canal worker

In addition to the problems they were facing with digging, Stevens and his team were also losing men right and left to Yellow Fever, the same mosquito-based pestilence that took more lives during the Spanish-American War than bullets did. It was an incredibly difficult illness to survive because it affected the blood's ability to clot, leading to internal bleeding. William Daniel Donadio, another descendant of a canal worker, noted, "The Yellow Fever. The fever attacking and killing everybody. The fever got everybody scared. Nobody wants to come to the isthmus to work."

Once someone contracted the virus, there was little anyone could do but provide palliative care and support while the body fought it off. Rose later described the effect of the illness on her daughter: "Her round face was pale, and the cold sweat stood out in beads all over her body. It was malaria and dysentery, and a dreary time we had of it. She became a limp, feverish little bundle, crying night and day. 'Keep everything sterile, and give her quinine,' cautioned the doctor. In that moldy atmosphere, it seemed impossible to keep dishes and linen sterile. The quinine, when I did get it down her little throat, made her sick at her stomach and she would lose it as fast I gave it to her. Sister did not respond to treatment to the doctor's satisfaction, and he talked of putting her in the hospital at Ancon. All the time I was becoming lower in spirits and less able to cope with the adverse conditions surrounding us. The thought of putting my baby in a strange hospital was the last straw. That night I gave way to old-fashioned screaming hysterics, outside beside the roaring cataract. Poor little Janey clung to me, her frightened eyes searching mine for the cause of such carryings on!"

The chief medical officer for the Panama Canal was a medical doctor named Colonel William Gorgas. Gorgas himself had survived an attack of Yellow Fever and had subsequently built his career around fighting it, to the point that he was one of the first men to understand the link between the illness and mosquitoes. While many believed there was nothing to his claims, he was fortunate enough to win the trust of Roosevelt's personal physician, who told his illustrious patient, "You are facing one of the greatest decisions of your career. If you fall back on the old methods you will fail, just as the French failed. If you back Gorgas, you will get your canal. This canal is your project and it's your choice." That was enough for Roosevelt, who instructed Stevens, "Get behind Gorgas and give him the authority and the resources he needs."

Gorgas

To their credit, the sanitation committee did all they could to combat what some called "the American Plague" once they understood what was causing it. Rose later wrote about their efforts: "From here every morning the sanitary gangs, accompanied by an inspector or boss, started out on their way to conquer the mosquito and the jungle. The quinine squad usually came first. Large bottles of bright red liquid were carried about and given in copious doses to all on the job. I was urged to give it to the children and to take it myself daily, but I could not bring myself to do it very often. Doubtless it did much to combat the ravages of malaria, but the very thought of it still has the power to send a shudder down my spine. After this gang came the oil gang. These men went out with small tanks of crude oil strapped to their shoulders. Hand pumps enabled them to spray all pools, streams, and puddles with the oil that would prevent the hatching out of mosquito eggs. Men with machetes cut down the brush, and others with shovels made ditches for drainage."

Gorgas also spent $90,000 on screening for the buildings in which the workers lived. Through his efforts, the number of new cases fell by half within just a few months, and by the end of 1906, the illness was all but gone.

With his workers now healthy and likely to stay that way, Stevens was able to focus his attention fully on digging the canal. This proved to be a good thing, especially when the president decided to make a visit to the site and see for himself how things were going. Calling a press conference to announce that he was about to become the first president to leave the country while in office, Roosevelt told reporters, "I want to see how they are going to dig that ditch, how they are going to build that lock; how they are going to get through that cut. It's a business trip. I want to be able to tell people as much as I can about the canal."

Arriving in Panama on November 14, 1906, Roosevelt quickly slipped past the formal welcome and made his way to the men's barracks, where he took time to speak with many of them personally. Donadio observed, "He made the men that were building there feel like they were special people. Give them pride of what they were doing for the United States." When it started pouring rain, he announced, "That's bully great to have so much rain," knowing it would give him a chance to see the operation under less than ideal conditions.

The trip was huge morale boost for both the workers and the United States. As Rose later recalled, "'In America, anything is possible,' Jan would boast, whenever he learned of some modern miracle of enterprise in his new country ... he was forever marveling at the spectacle of progress in the United States at the turn of the century, and from time to time he would add, proudly, 'With Teddy Roosevelt, anything is possible!' ... We saw him once, on the end of a train. Jan got small flags for the children, and told us about when the train would pass, so we were standing on the [front] steps. Mr. Roosevelt flashed us one of his well-known toothy smiles and waved his hat at the children as though he wanted to come up the hill and say 'Hello!' I caught some of Jan's confidence in the man. Maybe this ditch will get dug after all, I thought."

While in Panama, Roosevelt was in his element, freed from the chains of his White House desk. In fact, he surprised and delighted reporters by jumping aboard one of the giant steam shovels and operating it himself for a bit, creating one of the most famous photo-ops in American history.

A 1906 picture of Roosevelt sitting on a steam engine at a work site on the canal

Nonetheless, just a few short months after the president's triumphant visit, Stevens wrote to Roosevelt, "The 'honor' which is continually being held up as an incentive for being connected with this work, appeals to me but slightly. To me the canal is only a big ditch, and its great utility when completed, has never been so apparent to me, as it seems to be to others." With that,

Stevens resigned, thereby requiring Roosevelt to find a replacement to finish the canal.

Upset about losing yet another Chief Engineer, Roosevelt decided that he had to find someone who would not quit when the going got tough. Eventually, he appointed George Washington Goethals, one of the best engineers in the Army Corps and an expert in hydraulics. Rose described Goethals as "a tall, long-legged man with a rounded, bronzed face and snow-white hair. His moustache was also white, but slightly stained with nicotine, for he smoked many cigarettes. Except for his very erect carriage one would never have taken him for an army officer, for he never appeared in uniform. He wore civilian clothes with the usual awkwardness of a man who has spent most of his lifetime clothed in the uniform of his country."

Goethals

Sounding every bit like a military man, Goethals said of his new assignment, "It's a case of just plain straight duty."

The Old Man Was...On the Job

"It seemed that almost at once we could feel the effect of a strong, steady hand on the wheel. ... The Colonel [George Goethals], or the Old Man as he was soon nicknamed, seemed to be omnipresent. His routine was to be on the job from early morning until noon, and in his office all afternoon. ... I might see the Old Man, black umbrella hooked over one arm, climbing around in the Cut over loose rocks and dirt, stopping to watch a shovel or talk to a foreman or locomotive engineer, or making his way out to meet the car and go farther along the line to some other point of the job. The Old Man was so constantly on the job that we never thought of him as being at home or eating or sleeping. If he was ever sick, we did not know about it. As the men came to know him better, they found him to be fair and just at all times." - Rose van Hardeveld

Goethals quickly discovered that he had been thrown into the deep end of the pool. In March 1907, just a few weeks after his appointment, the steam shovel workers went out on strike and demanded a 40% pay increase. Since they were already among the highest paid workers on the project, Goethals refused their request and instead recruited other men to take their places, insisting "that defection by any one class of men could not tie up the whole work." This, and similar actions, earned Goethals the nickname "Czar of Panama." Detail-oriented and determined, he took control of every aspect of the project, from the hours the men worked to the food they could buy, and the result was a boon to those living and working in the area. Rose van Hardeveld remembered, "Jantje did bring us something wonderful from Panama. When he went into a wholesale importer's place he found them unpacking the first contingent of Edison phonographs that had ever been on the Isthmus. Jantje immediately bought two phonographs and a half dozen records for each. We had not realized how starved we were for music and entertainment until we heard the first strains of "Silver Threads Among the Gold" floating from the big tin horn. ... Now Jan sat entranced as he played the records over and over. Marina and I enjoyed the songs, while Jantje danced around with the baby in his arms to the music of Hungarian Rhapsody. We hung over the little box of a machine while supper, rain, canal, everything was forgotten for the time being. ... The promised commissary had become a reality: not much more than a shed, but gratifying accessible to me after these long months of having to travel long distances for food or do without. There were staples and canned goods, including milk, onions and potatoes and once in a great while a few pale shrunken cabbages. Greatest and best of all was American beef sent each morning from the cold storage plant at Cristobal. The urgently needed corrections and improvements in both living conditions and work on the canal project, which Jan had for so long confidently predicted, were at last materializing as the dry season drew to its close in 1907."

Though he knew that happy men were usually hardworking men, Goethals' main concern still lay in canal building, and he threw himself into constructing the locks that were needed on each side of the isthmus, as well as the damming of the Chagres. However, nothing was as vital as the canal itself, known locally as "the Cut." The Cut through the Culebra soon became a matter of intense focus, with 6,000 men working on it 24 hours a day every day of the week. More than 300 drills were constantly running, while 60 or more giant steam shovels dug out enough dirt and rock to keep more than 200 trains constantly occupied in carrying it away. Dynamite exploded, men cursed, and the temperatures regularly surpassed 110 degrees. Known by some as Hell's Gorge, it was one of the most dangerous places on the planet to work. Donadio explained, "They'd hear this tooting of the whistle. Blaring out, and they'd know that something went wrong, a slide. So they had to use pick and shovels to dig them out. They knew that a next slide could come down on them too and bury them too. The mountain didn't want to be crushed the way they did it, and the mountain fought back."

Of course, worker safety was not nearly the concern it is today. As Marco Mason pointed out, "There were no safety guidelines. There was no labor guidelines. Every day men died. It was a regular situation. So now they have to bring in more men and more men and more men. My grandfather told me the guys that go up front with the dynamite, that they would leave with their buddies their belongings, 'cause they never know if they are coming back up. It was a daily situation that today, this morning, you have breakfast, and somebody at that table having breakfast may not be there for that evening so it is that type of situation."

The slides in particular worried the workers and their families. Rose remembered that "the 'Cucaracha Slide, with all its accompanying minor slides, was getting in its harrowing work. The slides became an absorbing reality from now on. The men coming from or going to work would call to each other, 'How does she look today?' and, 'Cucaracha slid more dirt into the Cut last night than we can dig out in a month.'"

Eustace Tabois later described the dynamiting process: "They had to drill these holes, you know, through the rock. And after they get down to a certain depth they fill it with dynamite. Then when they are ready, they give you warning so that you go and take shelter." Granville Clarke, who also worked on the canal, added, "Three, four, five places start to blast. Big rocks going up in the air. What happens sometimes is somebody make a mistake and touch the wire and that guy is gone up too." Another worker, John Bowen, recalled one such accident: "It happened a Sunday morning when the pay car was there paying men. Pay car and all was in the explosion. A couple a hundred men, a couple a hundred men. Like you see bits of men here, and the head yonder, all those picking it up for days. Boy that wasn't an easy day, I tell you, Sunday morning."

In spite of the danger, the families of those working often visited the area and watched the progress from a safe distance. Rose explained, "We made it a habit to go once a week to the Cut to watch the progress made in the canal. We stood awed at the whining, groaning thing of iron, which obeyed so well the wishes of two men, its masters. Sometimes Jan took us and explained how the craneman controlled the leavers which caused the big dipper to drop and take huge bites out of the earth with its great, iron teeth; then swing around and from its hinged jaw spit all the contents out into the empty car which was waiting for it. He told us of the duties of the engineer who sat with his hands and feet ready at other levers, shifting, moving, controlling the different parts of the big machine. ... I tried to visualize the passengers and crews of the ships of the world that would proceed slowly and majestically through this canal when at last it was completed. Would they, thronging the deck and crowding the rails to watch their serene passage from one ocean to another, be aware of all the obstacles and hazards that had had to be overcome before their voyage could be made possible? Would they think, as they sailed from Atlantic to Pacific or from Pacific to Atlantic over the waters where once there had been only steaming jungle, of the long months of relentless excavation when banana trees sprang up in the midst of briefly neglected tracks?"

One of the reasons that the families were given the freedom to make such trips was that Goethals was trying very hard to keep his white workers happy. Prior to his arrival, most of the men whom came to work on the canal left within just a few months, so he set about creating comfortable living quarters for families, knowing that having the wives and children with them would make the men more likely to stay and less likely to get into trouble. Rose described these lodgings: "They were all alike, these dozen or fifteen cottages, painted battleship grey. They stood facing each other on either side of the road. A screened veranda across the front of the house; a living room and bedroom; then a hallway terminating in a clothes closet on one end and a pantry on the other; another bedroom; a dining room open on one side; and a kitchen finished the space in the structure. I appreciated the improvements I found here as compared to our dwelling on our private hill. The house was clean and comfortable, just about the type of home a man in the States would try to provide for his family. The roofs of corrugated tin came down low over the walls to shut out as much of the sun as possible. In the kitchen was the same small iron cook-stove, but a beautiful white porcelain sink with clean pipes over it was added, together with a table, two chairs, and plenty of shelves. To me, electricity was the greatest blessing. The quartermaster asked that we leave our porch lights on at night for street lamps. ... Now that families had arrived in the Zone in appreciable numbers, and homes were established where the men could be sure of their bath after work and a good breakfast before work and a comfortable place in which to relax, attendance in the saloons fell off to a considerable degree, and normal social patterns became possible."

Fully aware of the principle of "leading from the front," Goethals even brought his own family to the Canal Zone, leading Rose to later recall, "It delighted me that the wives of most of our officials were on the Isthmus with their husbands. I enjoyed seeing the tall, stately Mrs. Goethals and small, dainty Mrs. Gaillard going by ... or on the observation platform of a train. I knew that if we had an almost inedible tough roast for Sunday dinner, so did they, for they bought from the same shipment as we did; and if my husband got wet and muddy and cross, very likely theirs did too; and it pleased me to think that these wives of high-salaried men found their duties right by the side of their husbands, just as we all did. … We drew together in a sort of a compact clique. And nothing else seemed quite so important as this immense project moving gradually and steadily to completion. This was our life."

The Promise of Victory

"Despite my efforts to be calm and sensible, I found myself reviewing the weapons with which this land had fought back at us through the years. Pests and plagues… Relentless heat and incessant rains such as we white peoples had never been meant to withstand… Scarcities of wholesome food for the body, and of social and recreational nourishment for the spirit, as well… Creeping mold and fungus destroying our homes, ravaging hordes of insects destroying not only our garden produce and our kitchen supplies, but even our books, our clothing and linens. Throughout the years, now, we women had struggled against these threats to the preservation of the homes so necessary for the survival of all of us, while our men had gashed away at the miles and tons of earth we were so determined to conquer. The promise of victory loomed imminent – and now the land beneath us shuddered and quaked, menacingly it seemed… To remind us, I could not help wondering how vulnerable we still were, at the very moment of our triumph?" - Rose van Hardeveld

Gradually, and almost unconsciously, the workers were creating not just a canal but a little part of the United States in Central America. By 1911, newspapers all over the world were praising American progress on the canal, leading people from many different countries to plan visits to the area to see what one called "the greatest liberty ever taken with nature." Rose captured some of the sentiment at the time when she wrote, "The six or seven mile gash from Bas Obispo through Empire on a work day was really an awe-inspiring spectacle. Between forty and fifty huge shovels smoked and wangled at different elevations. Each shovel had its own short spur of track, then the track alongside for the dirt train. If blasting were necessary, there would be the drills churning up and down in the rock formation. There were the switches, the dynamite storage boxes, the network of wires for shooting, the engines snorting and puffing, the switchmen's shanties. To the casual eye this would all seem confusion and chaos. There were Spaniards carrying loads on their backs, others working with pick and shovel; there were Negroes carrying loads on their heads, or signaling engines or trains; water boys, errand boys, all moving in a seemingly conglomerate mass. There were white men here and there walking about, climbing over rock and piles of dirt, stopping here to give directions, there to inspect a piece of work. Engineers with sleeves rolled back, rolls of paper in their hands; time inspectors marking in their books, foremen flipping the sweat from dripping brows and yelling at their gangs; greasy, overalled trainmen and shovel men all moved by the same power, it would seem, each having a place in that Inferno, a place where his puny hands, together with the big machinery, worked to move, literally, a mountain from the path… A path that had, by the mind of man, been appointed to become a stairway to carry the ships of the world on their way from ocean to ocean. I stood many times on the bank gazing with fascination down into that hot teeming canyon and its scarring cuts. They seemed so puny against the task that loomed before them. Here, as nowhere in the world until now, was a living illustration of what the mind of man could accomplish when trained and directed."

Among the best aspects of seeing the canal, the locks were the greatest of all, and they came to be known as the "mighty portals to the Panama Gateway." That said, one man pointed out that they were, in reality, "incredibly elaborate culverts" that were created by using 5 million bags of concrete mixed and poured into multiple gigantic buckets, each holding six tons of concrete. Once loaded, each bucket was hoisted by a heavy cable and poured from above into the mold for the lock.

A picture of the Pedro Miguel Locks under construction

Since these were by far the largest locks ever built, those in charge did things a bit differently, including making the gates controlling them watertight but hollow so that they floated and therefore put less weight on the hinges. Though they were more than 80 feet tall, they were so light that they could be controlled by a 40 horsepower electric motor powered by a hydroelectric system located nearby. One man observed, "These locks are more than just tons of concrete. They are the answer of courage and faith to doubt and unbelief. In them are the blood and sinew of a great and hopeful nation, the fulfillment of ancient ideals and the promise of larger growth to come."

Rose also remembered seeing men work on the locks: "It was quite difficult to realize that there was other work than digging going in the canal construction. The big machine shops at Gorgona and the many men employed there composed another and still different unit of which I knew nothing beyond the fact that they took care of the machine repairs and such machine construction as was done on the Zone. On very infrequent passings by on the train we could see the huge forms, and knew that thousands of feet of concrete were being poured for the locks. We knew that an immense dam was being constructed at Gatun. I neglected my housework many times to walk to the edge of the Cut to watch the progress of the work and visualize the day when ships would be moving past this very hill on which I stood. Nothing else seemed quite so important as this immense project moving gradually and steadily to its completion. Nearly all the women and children felt the same way, and we would usually encounter our neighbors at one vantage point or another when we responded to the irresistible attraction of the dramatic view. This was our life. All other things were subordinate. To see water surging through this yawning canyon, ready to carry ships up and down its mighty locks, was the destiny which all our days and nights were shaped."

In May 1913, exactly nine years after they began, the Americans completed the Panama Canal when steam shovels 222 and 230 met in the middle of the Culebra Cut, each having completed a journey from their own respective coasts. A month later, the workers sealed the Gatun Dam and allowed the Gatun Lake to fill. Then, in August, the work dikes that had held the oceans back at either end of the canal were blown down, allowing water from the Atlantic and Pacific Oceans to rush in and eventually meet each other. Finally, on Monday, October 10, 1913, an enthusiastic crowd gathered near Gatun Lake to witness the final explosion that blew up the Gamboa Dike connecting Gatun Lake with the canal. Rose van Hardeveld described the scene: "We could easily see the dike with men still working around it. Not many yards to one side was the gash of the Cut, not very deep here. The small waves lapped eagerly at the edge, as though the lake was also waiting to let go some of its overload of water. … There was a reverent silence. No one spoke at all. There was a low rumble, a dull muffled B-O-O-M! A triple column shot high in the center, turned, and gracefully fell to both sides like a fountain. From the multitude came a spontaneous long, loud roar of such joy and relief that I felt sure I would remember the sound all my life. As the water poured out of the lake into the Cut, hats came off. We saw Jan and the engineer in charge of the Cut shake hands. They were both crying. We were crying, too."

Stan Shebs' picture of Gatun Lake

Of course, there were many tests to perform once the canal was operational. On August 3, 1914, just days after the start of World War I, America celebrated a triumph as the *Cristobal* made the first successful trip through the Panama Canal. Less than two weeks later, the canal was officially open for business. It had cost $350 million and countless lives, but the greatest symbol yet of America's power and prestige was complete, and the staggering accomplishment was summed up eloquently by one of Roosevelt's quotes: "It is not the critic who counts, not the man who points out how the strong man stumbled, or where the doer of deeds could have done them better. The credit belongs to the man who is actually in the arena; whose face is marred by dust and sweat and blood; who strives valiantly, who errs and comes short again and again; who knows the great enthusiasms, the great devotions, and spends himself in a worthy cause; who, at the best, knows in the end the triumph of high achievement; and who, at the worst, if he fails, at least fails while daring greatly, so that his place shall never be with those cold and timid souls who know neither victory nor defeat."

Jan van Hardeveld later received the Roosevelt Medal for his part in the canal's construction: "I couldn't help thinking of those who worked beside me who lost their lives. I thought of the many times when I nearly gave in to doubts that the Canal could ever be completed, that it was ever meant to be. But most of all, I was remembering how my answer to my own doubts, every time, was my faith in my country. I have always believed America could accomplish anything she set out to do."

Camilo Molina's picture of the Panama Canal near the Pacific entrance

The Hoover Dam

A Vision in the Desert

"Boulder Dam was, first of all, a vision in the desert. …in 1902 Arthur Powell Davis, having taken a civil engineering degree at Columbian University, and having spent several years as hydrographer with the abortive Nicaragua Canal Commission, began to make his own rich contribution to the Colorado's history. He studied the endless, mud-shwishing Gulliver sprawled across the sun-scorched wastes of the Southwest. Now it moved in perpetual twilight under precipices as terrifying as the cliffs of dream. Now it wound into remorseless sunlight between lonely rock horizons upon whose brows you half expected to see the stain of perspiration. Near the southern tip of Nevada the river entered Black Canyon. The walls of Black Canyon are considerably higher than the Woolworth Building and they diverge enough to be thoroughly baked by the sun. There is no hotter or more desolate scene on the Colorado - a turgid stream in a towering furnace of stone, a parching parody of all that the sweet word river has meant to the poets." – Excerpt from a 1933 article in *Fortune*

Since its inception, the Hoover Dam has been one of America's most controversial and powerful construction projects. In fact, its very name was controversial; the dam was originally named for Herbert Hoover, the president who initiated its construction, but it was later called the Boulder Dam when the former president fell out of favor with the American people. Of course, the Boulder Dam went back to being known as the Hoover Dam when time and history presented the much maligned president in a more positive light.

Hoover

However, before Hoover or any other president ever considered the idea, another, mostly forgotten man imagined what it could be. According to a 1933 article featured in *Fortune* magazine, "There in Black Canyon Arthur Powell Davis had his vision. For twenty succeeding years he gave his finest energies to the notion of the dam. Boulder Dam became a local and then a national issue. It involved scores of prominent Americans in disputes political, financial, and technical. But in the jagged valleys of the Colorado or in Washington or anywhere else there was no dispute about one fact: Boulder Dam was fundamentally the conception of Arthur Powell Davis; it was everlastingly based on his monumental engineering report."

Davis

A 1920s sketch of the proposed dam site and the resulting reservoir

That report was known as the Fall-Davis report, named after Davis and his co-author, then Interior Secretary Albert Fall. In their opinion, the Colorado River could be dammed up and used to generate a significant amount of electricity for the burgeoning population in the surrounding area, but they believed the federal government would have to take the lead in legislating its use since the river flowed through several states.

Fall

Davis had already proposed that the dam could be begun by blowing up the walls of Boulder Canyon and using whatever stone did not wash away to build it, and while that particular idea was not terribly popular, most agreed that some sort of dam should be built. However, the politics of the matter proved to be nearly insurmountable; according to *Fortune*, "In 1923 the wrangling got so hectic in the office of Secretary of the Interior Hubert Work that Mr. Davis resigned his positions as Director and Chief Engineer to the Reclamation Service. Gray and gentle and disillusioned, he went to California, where he worked on local aqueducts, and to Turkestan, where he was the Soviets' Chief Consulting Engineer on irrigation."

Meanwhile, others continued the fight, and by early 1930, with the country in the throes of an economic depression that only more jobs could cure, the federal government figured that thousands of men who were otherwise out of work could be sent west to southern Nevada to build a dam. Thus, on July 7, 1930, newspapers around the country received the following press release:

"The Secretary of the Interior announced today that construction of the Boulder Canyon project had commenced, immediately on the President's signature of the appropriation bill. The engineer in charge, Mr. Walker R. Young, and his assistants, were already on the ground waiting telegraphic instructions. The first day's work began the staking out of the railroad and the construction road, surveys of which have already been completed, laying out streets for the town site, and continuation of surveys for the water supply system. The order which started construction was signed by the Secretary immediately following the President's signature of the appropriation bill, and read as follows:

Order No. 436 Hon. Elwood Mead, Commissioner of Reclamation.

Sir: You are directed to commence construction on Boulder Dam today.

Respectfully, Ray Lyman Wilbur, Secretary.

The Secretary stated that the plans and specifications are being carried to completion with all possible expedition, looking to the advertising of bids and the awarding of construction contracts at the earliest possible date. Following the completion of the work begun today on the railroad, construction road, town site, and water works, the money appropriated will be used to commence construction of the cofferdams and diversion tunnels."

Wilbur also made a few public comments about the project, some of which reflected the perspective of the times but might offend modern environmental sensitivities: "The Boulder Dam will signalize our national conquest over the Great American Desert. With dollars, men, and engineering brains we will build a great natural resource. We will make new geography, and start a new era in the southwestern part of the United States. With Imperial Valley no longer menaced by floods, new hope and new financial credit will be given to one of the largest irrigation districts in the West. By increasing the water supply of Los Angeles and the surrounding cities, homes and industries are made possible for many millions of people. A great new source of power forecasts the opening of new mines and the creation of new industries in Arizona, Nevada, and California. To bring about this transformation requires a dam higher than any which the engineer has hitherto conceived or attempted to build."

Wilbur

Naturally, the project proved to be an immediate boost for the local community, as one woman recalled: "Now, Murl Emery had a ferry across the river before we ever began to build the dam, so all of the engineers that had been doing the surveying for everything knew Murl. He had the contract to take the men down the river in boats to the diversion tunnels. The diversion tunnels were being dug from both ends at the same time. That meant that there were 8 crews around the clock - - 24 crews a day - - going to those diversion tunnels, and they all went down river on the boats."

In addition to generating electricity, the main purpose of the Hoover Dam project was to generate jobs for those hit hardest by the Great Depression. In addition to workers, there would be need for an extensive support staff, including bookkeepers, grocery store workers, and even doctors and nurses. At the same time, however, Wilbur initially warned those desperate for jobs about what they were getting into if they decided to move to Nevada: "Of one thing the public should be warned and that is the unwisdom of going to the vicinity of the dam site in the expectation of getting work without ample provision to meet the emergency should this expectation fail. The dam site is located in the midst of a great desert with few inhabitants and slight opportunity for other employment than that which it may afford. Employment will develop only as contracts are let and ample notice will be given when opportunities for work present themselves."

Despite the official caveats, as one article pointed out, the Hoover Dam was as much a political triumph as it was an engineering feat: "Boulder Dam will not only be a monumental engineering work, but the laws authorizing it inaugurated the greatest scheme of rural planning yet undertaken in the West. That this scheme shall prove of the greatest possible value to the Nation, it necessitates now a study of all irrigation and power possibilities of the whole basin, and of the different States. Five hundred thousand dollars has been provided this year for studies of secondary projects in the Colorado Basin. This includes $100,000 for a study of the irrigation possibilities of Utah, Colorado, Wyoming, and New Mexico, the four States above Boulder Dam; $250,000 for surveys and preparation of plans and estimates for the Parker-Gila project in Arizona; and $150,000 for continuing the surveys and preparation of plans and estimates for the Palo Verde, Imperial, and Coachella Valleys. Altogether, these investigations will deal with the possible future reclamation of 6,000,000 acres of land, an area equal to that now irrigated in the lower Nile. Consideration must be given to a possible 6,000,000 horsepower electrical development on the river as a whole."

And what of Davis? According to the 1933 article in Fortune, "For ten years Boulder Dam proceeded without him. The money was at long last appropriated, actual blasting was begun. In California, far from these detonations, Mr. Davis' health began to fail. The Prosperity Party changed the name of the project to Hoover Dam. Mr. Davis' name, which had never had much advertisement in the first place, dropped out of memory as quickly as that of any ill and retired American. On June first of this year the first buckets of concrete were poured into the hugest mold ever conceived; the Colorado already writhed helplessly in a strait-jacket of stone and steel. At length in mid-July the forgotten Mr. Davis received his own particular New Deal. The new Administration concluded perhaps that just dues were better late than never, and Mr. Davis appointment as consulting Engineer on Boulder Dam was announced by Secretary Ickes. And at seventy-two Arthur Powell Davis returned, or was returned, to his vision. His health was too delicate to permit much actual field work in the Molochian jaws of Black Canyon. But on the Washington records he was back at what any of the boys on the canyon will be first to admit was his job."

Whatever joy Davis had at seeing his vision start to become reality, it was short lived. He died just a few months later, long before the dam was ever completed.

The Six Companies

"The Boulder Canyon Project Act authorized federal appropriations not to exceed $165,000,000. They were apportioned as follows:

Dam and reservoir $70,600,000
Power development 38,200,000
All-American Canal 38,500,000
Interest during construction 17,700,000

One hundred and sixty is fair candy money, even for Washington. And particularly when forty-five states in the Union are not getting so much as a gumdrop. The sullen watchfulness of eastern, southern, northern, and mid-western Congressmen made a waste-proof spending plan imperative. Two set-ups were possible. The dam could be government built (cries of "No! No! The government will lose money!"). The dam could be built on private contract (cries of "No! No! The government will lose money!"). The problem was solved by compromise. The dam is under the direct supervision of the Washington and Denver offices of the U.S. Government's Bureau of Reclamation; actual designs of all its features are made in the Denver office. It is being built by a group of western contractors, calling themselves the Six Companies." – Excerpt from a 1933 article in *Fortune*

When the Federal government announced the scale of the project and its budget, companies from all over the country sat up and took notice. As the 1933 *Fortune* article proclaimed, "When Washington announced it had the job for somebody, a sudden low scribbling was heard in the land. This was the sound of estimating. Most of it died very quickly, as contractors realized the job was too huge even to bid on."

Not only was the job itself big, but in order to limit competition to only those companies who were likely large enough to see the dam completed, the government insisted that the winning bidder put up a $5 million completion bond that would be forfeited if they quit before the project was finished. In reality, no company in Depression-era America could afford to risk that kind of money. As the article continued, "But in San Francisco, Salt Lake City, Boise, and Portland, telephones jangled and very quickly the hard heads of Bechtel & Kaiser and MacDonald & Kahn (San Francisco), Morrison-Knudson Co. (Boise), Utah Construction Co. (Salt Lake City), and Portland's J.F. Shea and the Pacific Bridge Co. were put together. They set up a joint corporation capitalized for $8,000,000, called it the Six Companies, scribbled, estimated, and bid $48,890,995, bonded the contract for $5,000,000 in cash. They got the job."

And what a job it was. The article explained, "For their $48,890,995 the Six Companies must foot all construction bills - for dynamite, for trucks, for digging mud and dumping mud, for bosses' salaries, and for labor's wage. The Six companies do not pay for construction raw material - for the 5,500,000 barrels of cement consumed, or the 55,000 tons of steel plates and castings, or the turbines and generators in the power plant, or any of the permanent operating machinery of the dam. ... They were out of pocket $3,500,000 for preliminary work before they received a government penny. Until half the work was done they received only ninety cents on the dollar. The holdback is around $2,000,000, which they will receive at the end - like an ice-cream cone for being good. It suffices perhaps to say that during the first five months of 1933 the government paid an average monthly bill from the Six Companies of $1,513,000. Out of this the corporation must pay items such as a half-million a month payroll, $48,000 for gas and oil, $40,000 for electricity. At one time when the roads were roughest, they were spending $500 a day for truck and automobile tires. When the last bills are paid and the turbines begin to turn, the Six companies will have turned a profit estimated at $7,000,000 and upward for all their work."

One of the most daunting questions about building the dam was related not to engineering but to managing the workforce that would prove to be an integral part of its construction. Wilbur knew this and pointed out early on that the dam "is to be built in a region of intense summer heat, amid desert surroundings and where the public lands, in large part, are being surveyed for the first time. To build the dam economically and efficiently requires that special attention be given to those factors which influence the health and energy of the workers." This was a wise and necessary move, as the American desert and Badlands had already taken the lives of hundreds of men, women and children more rugged and prepared for hard living than those folks coming to work on the dam.

To make sure that all was done to prepare an environment conducive to productivity, Wilbur proposed the following plan: "A thousand men will be employed over a period of five to eight years. Many of these will have families, and this means that the town to be created near the dam site will have a population of 4,000 to 5,000 people. This town will not be a temporary construction camp. During the time that the dam is under construction, thousands of tourists will each year visit this section. When it has been completed, the lake 100 miles in length above it will draw other thousands because of its scenic beauties. Plans accordingly have been made to lay out a town which will represent the most modern ideas in town planning. The water works will be similar in character to those built at Yuma, Ariz., where the conditions of climate and water are similar to those at Boulder Dam. From the town site to the dam is about three miles. The town will be connected with the outside world by an automobile road and a railroad about 30 miles in length. ... Of the initial appropriation of $10,660,000, $2,500,000 will be used to build the railroad, $525,000 will be expended in the construction of waterworks, laying out the town, building streets, sewers, and other conveniences of the town, and in the construction of a main office building for the Government engineers and clerical staff and 25 homes for its permanent employees at the dam. ... In preparation for the project, the government built a new, planned community in the desert. Known as Boulder City, Nevada, it was connected by rail to the Union Pacific Railroad on September 17, 1930. Construction on the dam officially began less than two weeks later, on September 30."

While what Wilbur described was the ultimate goal, he knew all too well that it was not a good idea to sit on money that had already been appropriated by Congress for too long, so he made clear that it was "not necessary that construction of the tunnels to divert the river shall await the completion of these facilities of living and transportation. There is a good road from Las Vegas to the canyon. ... A temporary construction camp can be located on the river and the construction of the tunnels thereby expedited."

As a result, the community that the government first constructed was far from Wilbur's ideal. In fact, it was probably only the desperate times that compelled anyone to be willing to live there. According to Emma Godbey, who moved into "Ragtown" with her family in 1931, "We lived in a tent in the river bottom. We bought this tent from a widow whose husband had been disemboweled by a shovel handle when he had gone in to muck out after a blast that hadn't completely blown yet. ... We also had to get another tent. That tent was the one I cooked and we ate in. Then, we got another tent to sleep in. Between the tents, we spread blankets fastened to clothesline ropes with horse blanket pins so as to make a little shade for the children, because it was so hot down there. We bathed in the river. Of course, that meant that everybody had to wear some kind of apron or a little shift or something, and bathe the best they could. They dug some wells a little ways back from the river, but I saw that dirty looking utensils were being dipped into the wells until I was afraid to use the water. Of course, people had to use their utensils on campfires to cook. I told my husband that I just couldn't see drinking the water out of the wells. The water from the river, although it was pure, was so full of silt that you'd have to leave it to settle before you could drink it. He would get water from the mess halls for the road crew camp."

Canyon Work

"Year in, year out, Crowe and Young and their 200-odd inspectors and foremen and their labor gang battle the Colorado twenty-four hours a day. The day shift comes on at 7:00 A. M. and knocks off at 3:00 P. M. Swing shift from 3:00 P. M. to 11:00 P. M. Graveyard from 11:00 P. M. to 7:00 A. M. The inevitably ribald slang of the construction camp has coined for the wives of the night workers the name of 'Graveyard Widows.' At night Black Canyon is lighted like a theatre with incredible clusters of sun arcs, bought from a bankrupt San Francisco ball park. The men come to work in covered lorries wearing papier-mache safety helmets that look like A. E. F. tin hats [The American Expeditionary Force was the force deployed to Europe in World War I]. These serve to protect them from falling rock--the greatest danger of the canyon work. Despite this precaution, in addition to a doctor and a field hospital at the base of the dam, over fifty men had given their lives to Boulder Dam by midsummer last year [1932]." – Excerpt from a 1933 article in *Fortune*

General Superintendent Frank Crowe (right) and Bureau of Reclamation Engineer Walter Young at the site

John Cahlan, one of the men who worked on the project, was quick to note "that before they could start the actual construction of Boulder Dam, there were two other major contracts that had to be completed. One was the road from Boulder City to the dam site; and the second was a railroad line from the Union Pacific Railroad out to Boulder City. That is the spur line that took off the Union Pacific main line about ten miles south of Las Vegas and went out to Boulder City. The railroad line is still in service, and the Union Pacific is servicing Henderson with that Boulder City line. At that time, there was no paved highway between Las Vegas and Boulder City. It was a dirt road and was nothing more than just a place cleared out, between here and Boulder City, so the cars could drive, if necessary. As they drove, ruts were dug into the dirt, about a foot or a foot and a half deep. You got your tires in the ruts, and that's where you had to stay. If somebody came along in the other direction, it was a major project to get one of the automobiles out of the rut so that the other one could pass it. But in 1932 the highway department put in a two-lane paved road which generally follows the same road that is there today."

In addition to working on the necessary transportation, the first step toward actually building the dam was to dig a number of large tunnels to divert the water of the Colorado River around the area where the dam would be built. According to Wilbur, "These diversion tunnels will be four in number, each 50 feet in diameter. Because of their size, their excavation will be very much like the operation of a quarry. The greatest problem will be the disposal of the excavated material. Part of it will be needed to build the cofferdams that will be placed in the river, above and below the site of the dam, to keep the water out of the excavation where the foundation of the dam is to be placed. The building of the road, the railroad, the tunnels, and the coffer dams will all precede the beginning of the great wedge, over 700 feet high, that is to close this river. While these earlier works are being built the final detailed plans for the dam will be completed."

Though he tried to explain the project in layman's terms, the Wilbur was aware that neither he nor most of his constituents would ever be able to fully grasp the planning and scientific calculations that went into the project. In fact, he once said, "Only engineers who have had considerable familiarity with dams and power development can fully appreciate all that is involved in these plans. The dam is not merely a mass of concrete to hold the water back. It is a complex industrial structure traversed by pipes and corridors, in which will be placed the regulating gates and the valves for the dynamos which will generate a million horsepower of electrical energy and the waste ways for controlling floods."

A picture of people touring the Hoover Dam's generators

A picture of a penstock used to transfer water to the Hoover Dam's turbines

A picture of some of the Hoover Dam's turbines

Another author focused on the sheer magnitude of the structure, a size that would ensure it a place on the list of history's greatest man-made marvels. He described it as "a concrete-arch, gravity-type dam which will tower 730 feet from canyon bedrock--almost as high as the…Woolworth Building. The base width will equal two city blocks. It will measure not much less than a quarter-mile across the top. The concrete used would build a standard sixteen-foot highway from Pensacola to Seattle--if you can visualize that. When complete it will back up the largest artificial body of water in the world, sufficient to cover Connecticut to a depth of ten feet. This will form a grimly beautiful lake 115 miles long and full of tourist steamboats."

According to an investigation by *Fortune* magazine, "Boulder Dam has four purposes," with the first one being "flood control." As the author reminded readers, the river it was damming up, while mighty and beautiful, also had a reputation for being treacherous to the surrounding area. The article explained, "The yellow Colorado water has for many years watered the rich desert farms of southern California and western Arizona. Often it flooded them, sweeping away budding crops, farmers' fords, and the farmers themselves. Boulder Dam will not only block the largest flood on record but it will hold almost two full years' flow behind its bulk, releasing a normal stream throughout the year. A sub-purpose is silt removal, whereby the muddy content will precipitate above the dam, simplifying and cheapening distribution to irrigation lands. Flood and silt have cost Southwest ranchers an estimated $2,000,000 yearly. This bill will have been paid for the last time when the Colorado, for the first time in thousands of years, flows evenly and clear to the Gulf."

In spite of the promise that the river would be safe, many preferred it untamed and in its natural state. Photographer W. A. Davis later complained, "I loved that old river. It was beautiful. I'd swam the river, I'd boated the river, I'd taken people up the river on trips...I felt bad to see it tamed, to tell you the truth."

The second purpose of the dam was "water conservation," since, according to the author writing in 1933, "Below the dam the Colorado now irrigates 660,000 acres of land. This acreage is limited by the low water flow. By storing spring floods, from five to seven times as much water will be available in summer, permitting irrigation on about 1,500,000 acres of new land 2,160.000 acres in all." As Blaine Hamann of the U.S. Bureau of Reclamation pointed out, "The river was an enemy, and only in short periods of time could you look at it as a useful river. Most of the time it was something that would kill you or ruin your farm."

The dam's third purpose was to supply water for "The Metropolitan Water District, comprising many cities and towns in southern California - principally Los Angeles." In fact, by 1933, those cities had already "contracted to take about a billion gallons daily from the river to wash southern California faces and water southern California lawns." According to one article, the "$220,000,000 aqueduct...will pay the U. S. about $250,000 yearly."

The final and most perhaps most obvious purpose of the dam was to supply electricity. As the author pointed out, "Under the mighty shadow of the dam will be built the biggest power plant in the world. This will develop 1,800,000 horsepower four times Niagara's power, thrice the ultimate capacity of Muscle Shoals. Already the electricity has been sold on fifty-year contracts to the city of Los Angeles and the Southern California Edison Co., which in turn subcontract 79 per cent of it (on percentages fixed by law) to Arizona, Nevada, the Metropolitan Water District, and smaller California valley towns."

Of course, the dam would cost people much more than money, as Wilbur pointed out when he said, "The greater part of the 150,000 acres which will be flooded is public land, but scattered through it are small areas of privately owned land, the largest one being in the valley of the

Virgin River." Though the population was scarce around the Boulder area at that time, many farmers and ranchers had to be uprooted from their home.

Naturally, nobody would ever fully understand the dam like the men who worked on it. One of them described some of the necessary tasks: "Now, a mucker was the one that had to clean the rock surface before the concrete was poured. This had to be clean enough so that you could practically eat off of it. Well, we did this for a while, and then I got a little better job: we went to concrete puddling. This is where you wore hip boots, you know, and a hard hat. They'd pour the concrete, and it was up to you to get it spread out with your feet. You had to work it pretty good, or you'd leave rock pockets. And you didn't dare do these because if you did, they had to be taken out and the space filled. This was hard work, you know. I was back in the various tunnels all this time, and they finally started pulling the plug, I think, in the number 2 tunnel on the Arizona side. At that time they put a monorail across the top of the main tunnel; then they could bring agitators full of concrete down on the main high line and set them on trucks. The trucks would back into this monorail, and there they would be picked up. I would hook them up and unhook them, just as a hook tender, and they would be monorailed back to where they needed the concrete."

After working on the tunnels for a awhile, that same worker admitted, "Well, of course, I still wanted a better job. So I asked Virginia Steelworkers, which at the time was tying all this reinforcing steel that went into all the walls of the various sections of the power house. And I got a job working for Herb Merner, who was the superintendent." This proved to be a good move, as he later recalled, "And so I tied steel. I went from...when I first went down there to the site as a laborer it was $4 a day, and then hook tender was $4.50 a day. Then I went to the steel crew at $5 a day. I finally got $5.60 a day tying steel. Well, when they finished pouring the plugs, and they started putting the penstocks in, too, why, it was up to the steelworkers to get the steel into these cradles that held the penstocks in place. All the steel was laid on top of the power house, and it was up to 2 or 3 of us to get ahold of one of these...oh, about 30-foot pieces of inch-and-a-quarter steel in a semicircle and get it through a small tunnel back to where they were used. Well, the journeymen $6-a-day men and the other $5.60-a-day men, myself included, were all doing the same work. So I asked Herb; I says, 'I want a raise. I want to get the same money they're getting.' He said, 'Young man, I'll pay a man for what they know, not for being you.' And so I worked on and kept pouring."

Young and Crowe

A picture of ongoing construction

A picture of workers working on the power plants

"There are two reasons why Young and Crowe are not bitter enemies. One is that the job is too big for petty human friction. Young's inspectors and Crowe's foremen know this as well as their bosses. They know that friction which slows work quietly rubs somebody out of a job. The second reason is the mutual respect of Young and Crowe. Crowe spent years in the U.S. Reclamation Service, which Young now represents. He knows Young's duties and responsibility as well as Young does. 'I'd go to hell for him,' says Crowe. Frank Crowe, according to close guessers at the dam, gets $25,000 a year plus bonuses. Young gets $6,375. And this government work rates no bonus, there being no American Legion of the Reclamation Service. But regardless of salary, Walker Rollo Young is the boss at Boulder Dam. The U.S. hired the Six Companies, who hired Crowe. The U.S. flag flies just outside Young's office window." – Excerpt from a 1933 article in *Fortune*

One historian has called Frank Crowe the Six Companies' "ace in the hole." According to one article written in the early months of the dam's development, "Walker Young helped design the dam and is on hand to see that it rises exactly according to specifications. But the man who is actually building it, probably the best man for the job in the world, is Frank T. Crowe. He has been called the Colonel Goethals of Boulder Dam. ... Frank Crowe ... twists around in a chair a lot while he talks, preferring the outdoors, and makes an absolute rule that no letter shall go out of his office over one page long. He believes any idea can be expressed in that space and that anything longer is a waste of words. He had one dominant desire in life--to work on dams--and has gratified that desire almost steadily since Arrowrock. He was U.S. Construction Engineer on the Tieton Dam in Washington and General Superintendent of the Jackson Lake Dam in Wyoming. For private contractors he built the Guernsey Dam on North Platte and Combre Dam on Bear River, California. His last job was the Deadwood Dam in Idaho, which began by walking with his construction gang through seventy miles of snow."

Crowe was the General Superintendent hired to see to it that the dam got built as quickly and efficiently as possible. A man who preferred to see his hands smeared with mud rather than ink, he lived by the motto "Never my belly to a desk." A graduate of the University of Maine, he had worked for the Reclamation service for most of his life when he learned that a number of dams in the west were to be built by private contractors. Unwilling to miss out on the fun, he gave up his position with the Reclamation Service and went to work for a private company. When he heard about the Hoover Dam project, he recalled, "I was wild to build this dam. I had spent my life in the river bottoms, and (Hoover) meant a wonderful climax—the biggest dam ever built by anyone, anywhere."

Given that background, the Six Companies looked over his resume and the man himself and put him in charge. According to the same article, "He has one hobby-the development of men; specifically, the men who follow him by hundreds to work on his dams His principal exhibit is Bernard (Woody) Williams, who first worked for him at thirteen, and now, at thirty, is in complete charge when Crowe leaves Black Canyon for Boulder City. For Williams and his foremen he has only one working rule: 'To hell with excuses–get results!' He is tall, talks loudly, and laughs hard. He is noted for his humor. ... He knows thousands of construction laborers by their first names and 'generally how many kids they got.' ... He is down in Black Canyon most of the day and often part of the night. ... He conveys an irresistible impression of drive, and translates it into almost magical results. The men dislike to work that hard, but they like Crowe. They work that hard."

Elton Garrett, one of the men who worked for him, agreed with that description's sentiments: "Frank Crowe was a genius for organized thinking and for imparting organized thinking to other people... He not only was an engineering genius, he was a people genius. That went a long ways." Another worker, Red Wixson, later remembered, "He didn't want to listen to what was going on down there. He wanted to see it with his own eyes. I never saw him get excited about anything. If something went wrong, he was there to get an eye on it, to explain what was wrong, fix it. He was there to help you, not to fire you. One thing he knew was men. ... He respected his men. He was appreciative."

In spite of his good relationship with his men, Crowe was no pushover, which became apparent when the workers went out on strike in August 1931. According to Leo Dunbar, "[W]hen the Wobblies [Industrial Workers of the World] got in here and tried to get a strike going, there was plenty of trouble. Mr. [Sims] Ely [the Boulder City manager] was very strict about those things. He had a good set of rangers who took care of the job and did the work. Of course, that was one reason that the government decided to move everybody out who wasn't employed at that time." The workers felt that they were not being paid enough for the dangerous and unpleasant work they were being called upon to do, but Crowe felt they were being unreasonable and declared, "The workers will have to work under our conditions, or not at all." In a nation with double digit unemployment, he had the clout to make this stick, and the strike ended in a week.

For all that the dam was being built by private contractors, it was still a government project, and the other man wielding power in the project was Walter Young of the Reclamation Bureau. According to Crowe, he and Young "like to cry at each other and raise hell. He says my foremen are no good, but he don't mean anything." When asked about this, Young agreed, saying, "Yes, sometimes we fight with each other for the fun of it."

One article described Young's background: "The engineering career of this quiet, sharp-eyed man who at forty-eight is commander of the government guard at Boulder Dam began at the University of Idaho. He studied mining, in addition to working most of his way through, captaining the basketball team, and presiding over the student body. He…took a government job as a designer on the construction of Idaho's Arrowrock Dam, the Boulder Dam of its time. On this job he met Frank Crowe, bossing a shift for the head engineer. From that day to this he has worked in the Reclamation Service as field investigator, designer, administrator. He has figured hydraulics on more dams than he call remember, twenty five of them on the Colorado alone-- ghost dams which never rose from mounds of paper. He contributed materially to the first and basic designs for Boulder Dam. He wears glasses, and hasn't smoked for months. … He regards engineering as an art--"The Art of Economical Construction." Combined with his great talents both as a designer and administrator is his ability to make big decisions and small ones with equal speed."

According to the article, Young also played a crucial part in the strike: "When the fearful heat of the first summer at Boulder and the lack of proper accommodations combined to brew a riot, he met it by ordering everybody off the U. S. Reservation. Then he invited every man who wanted to work to come back, assuring him of the best possible living conditions in the shortest possible time. The men came back. Of course, what they came back to was another matter, and while the housing might have been improved, their dangerous job was made more so by the rush to complete the project ahead of schedule.

In addition to Young and Crowe, there were a number of other men leading the project. As Wilbur pointed out, "The Reclamation Bureau will have the cooperation of the engineers of the

Los Angeles Water and Power Department and the Southern California Edison Co. and its related companies. … Its chief designing engineer, J. L. Savage, is recognized as a genius in his line. He has successively designed three dams which at the time of their construction were the highest in the world. …In addition to the corps of experts on the permanent staff of the bureau, it has as consulting engineers, A. J. Wiley, who has an international reputation and is consulting engineer for the irrigation department of India; L. C. Hill, the designer and resident engineer on the Roosevelt Dam and many monumental works in this and other countries; and D. C. Henny, one of the foremost consulting engineers of the country. Because of the exceptional size of the dam and the difficult engineering problems involved, Congress thought it prudent to create a board of five — three engineers and two geologists — who would review the plans and estimates prepared by the Bureau of Reclamation and report direct to the President. The engineers on this board — Gen. Wm. L. Seibert, builder of Gatun Locks at Panama, Darnel W. Mead, and Robert Ridgway — have approved all of the work thus far sub mitted to them, and will pass judgment on the detailed plans of the dam when these have been completed."

The Boulder Dam Worker

Pictures of workers

"The Boulder Dam worker of 1933 is a national type of some importance. He is a tough itinerant American--the 'construction stiff.' His average age is thirty-three. His average wage is sixty-eight cents an hour. He is taller and heavier than the average U. S. soldier, runs a greater risk of losing his life, and has passed a more drastic physical examination. He has been in most of the states of the Union and can find his Way in a dozen different kinds of unskilled and semi-skilled labor--a hoist in a Pennsylvania coal mine, a saw in Oregon, a shovel on a dozen road jobs. He has boiled a string of mules in Bluejacket, Oklahoma - followed a pipe line as it crept across a prairie, a few yards a day, toward a town invisible behind a hill range. He is inured to ceaseless, frightful heat--and fearful cold, too, for that matter. Four or five of him in an old car can always get to a row of lights on Saturday night and if some four-flusher cops his roll or his girl it may be a fight or a laugh-what's the difference?" – Excerpt from a 1933 article in *Fortune*

By 1933, the work on the dam was well underway, and thousands of people had pulled up stakes and moved to the desert in search of a job. Leo Dunbar was one of the married men who came to Boulder City with their families, and he remembered, "My wife and I had 3 small children…. The government had shipped my furnishings and everything we had down, and it was deposited in a brick house on Denver Street that had just been finished. Now, the plaster was wet, and everything was soaking, and, of course, they put the bedding on the floor in the living room and all the rest of the furniture on top of the bedding. I had been living in the camp on the site of what is now Lakeview. And after the family came down, some of the boys from the camp said, "Well, we'll help you get going." There was no heat in the house; we couldn't use electricity for heat, but there was an electric range that had just been installed. … The next thing was to make ourselves beds. So what we did was we lighted the range and used the oven in the range, went out and found a bunch of big rocks, put them in the range and warmed them. And we wrapped them up in papers and put them in the beds at night. And that was my hardship in coming here. But I was lucky to have a job, and my work went on from there."

For many people from other parts of the country, the environment itself was the most difficult thing to get used to. After all, Hoover Dam was built in the middle of a desert, and the area was chosen in part because it was so unpopulated, due to the fact few people wanted to live there. Marion Allen, one of the workers, recalled, "This little house down there on Seventh Street, what the wife kicked about, the sand come in off the desert, and the floor would get about a half inch deep of sand, you know. She'd sweep it out; by the time she got it swept out, it would move back in. … We lived there in that house pretty near 4 years. Rent was enormous; it was $15 a month. I think we paid $2 a month for water, but there was a restriction on that water- -you didn't water a yard, not even a green plant out there. If you did that, they'd be right down and they'd give you trouble and charge you double, which would be about $4, which wouldn't have been bad, but the second time, that was it. But they didn't kick about you running the water all night on the roof. And that was our cooling system. We'd fix the hose so it'd spray the roof and run down over the burlap canvas. That made our cooling. So that worked out pretty good. Otherwise, the worst thing we had to contend with was the heat- -trying to sleep. About the time you'd cool off a little- -about 6:00, 6:30 or 7:00 in the morning -- you had to be on the bus going to work. So as far as I was concerned, that was the hardest part of it. Otherwise, we were probably some of the fortunate ones. The other people that lived in the camps in tents and all- -who didn't have any refrigeration and very little water- -probably suffered a lot more."

Most of the families coming to Boulder had no idea how to cope with the living conditions there. Erma Godbey told of one particularly disturbing event: "Then I just got a terrible, terrible burn. My face was sunburned; it was windburned; it was campfire burned - - all 3. And I thought I'd caught some kind of a disease in the river. I was so afraid my children might get it that I . . . anybody that went into Vegas, I'd have them get me some Listerine and some cotton. And I was taking this pure Listerine and this cotton and dabbing my face, so I was drying it out and burning it with the Listerine as well as what was already there. It was just getting so terrible, I said to my husband, 'I've got to go to a doctor and see what's the matter with my face.' And he would laugh at me, because when I would change expression, I'd get little cracks, and they'd bleed. ... So, we made the trip to Las Vegas, and needless to say, there wasn't any highway. It was just up hills and down dale and in the arroyos and stuff and dust…the minute I opened the door and went into the doctor's office, he took one look at me, and he said, 'My God, woman! You've got the worst case of desert sunburn and windburn I've ever seen in my life!' ... Men used to go without a shirt, and then they would get such blisters on their back that sometimes they would be festered. And babies, especially - - people thought that they'd be cooler if they run around without anything, and they'd get these terrible sun blisters, and then they would open, and they would be infected."

Ironically, the housing project for the workers was built on a reservation formerly set aside by the government for use by Native Americans. It was also a highly controlled environment, as described by one author: "The gang on the job varies with the various steps in the dam's progress. The maximum estimated, but never reached, was 4,000 ... They eat and sleep in Boulder City, built on a U.S. reservation. Nobody call build houses or sell so much as a radish without a U.S. permit. And 80 per cent of the workers must live on the reservation."

This housing situation was made all the more ironic by the fact that the Hoover Dam was designed to help create the modern American West. The power it produced would allow a little town called Los Angeles to become one of the biggest cities in the world, and the men who built it would see another little town grow into a full-fledged tourist destination that had a seedy reputation even back then. As *Fortune* pointed out, "Las Vegas is a Nevada town twenty-three miles away, where drinking, gambling, and all the grosser forms of self-expression flourish."

Getting the men from their homes to the dam was a primary concern, and to accomplish this in the most organized way possible, the builders brought in large buses known as "transports." According to Mary Ann Merrill, whose husband worked on the dam, "They had a 2 decker, and they had different sized transports. They transported them all down there. [They would gather] up about Arizona Street and the Nevada Highway, because it seems to me I remember them getting off up there...where the bus came in, probably. But they had dormitories and the mess hall. Anderson had that on the west end of town, and they probably took the buses from there also. … They just took them down there. Some of them went on down below; some of them on top, of course, according to where you were working on the dam."

Not surprisingly, working conditions were terrible. Godbey recalled, "The men would go to work, and so many of the men were passing out with heat stroke that they decided that they would go to work at 4:00 in the morning and work until noon. Nobody worked from noon until 4:00 p.m. because that was the heat of the day. Another crew come on at 4:00 and worked till midnight with searchlights. At that time they didn't know anything about taking extra salt, and people were sweating out all the salt in their bloodstream, and they were passing out. … Now, this was the Depression, and so many men had walked miles and miles, and they had been without food also. So we had to go into Las Vegas. But you couldn't go into Las Vegas until you set a car in the river for 3 days. All the cars had wooden spokes in those days, and the spokes dried out so bad that they just rattled and came loose. So if you were going to go to Las Vegas, you had to set your car in the river, and then you had to move it a little bit - - not enough so as it'd float down the river, but enough so as the spokes would soak up - - before you could go into Las Vegas."

Over time, Boulder City grew and became more and more "civilized," but it was up to the residents to make many of the improvements they wanted to see. One woman explained, "At first, we didn't have any schools. There was no schools in Boulder at all, and so older kids had to go to Las Vegas to school, if they could get in there. Then they used 3 of the first Six Company houses built- -they were down fairly close to the El Rancho Motel, down in there- -and they used those for school buildings. Different women here in town who had taught school before they had come to Boulder City volunteered to teach. And people would pay a dollar and a half- -I don't know whether it was a week or a month- -per child. (I think it was a month.) And if they had 2 children, why, the second child was a dollar. There were no books or anything. They just had to do the best they could. Then, of course, we all raised cain because we didn't have any school. But this was a reservation; it wasn't a part of the state of Nevada. And so then we did get started to build a school. The first school was a brick building, which is now our city hall, and it didn't get finished until the latter part of September of 1932. The Six Companies contacted the school district in Las Vegas, and they told them what books they would need, and they kept them in their store. The people had to buy books for the children, and the school just didn't have any equipment at all. They had to do so much using the gelatin and making papers from the books for the kids to study from because there was never enough books in the Six Companies Store for the people even to buy when they could buy. It was about 3 years later when the state bought the books back from us. But, at first, the government built the building, and Six Companies hired the teachers. But we did go by the curriculum of the state of Nevada."

Thinking in Giant Terms

"Accustomed to thinking in giant terms they are not particularly moved because the dam has been given a new label by the Roosevelt Administration. The reversion of the name from Hoover Dam to Boulder Dam is considered around Black Canyon as politics. It is unofficially estimated that the shift may cost the U.S. some $200,000 in printing bills to change the staggering mass of documentary record that a dam entails. But that is no concern of the builders. Their world is bounded by the desert mountains and their lives are for the current years dedicated to a job." – Excerpt from a 1933 article in *Fortune*

In 1933, the new Secretary of the Interior, a Roosevelt appointee named Harold Ickes, issued an announcement that the Hoover Dam would become officially known as the Boulder Dam. While he did not admit this publicly, Ickes held a grudge against Hoover, the man his boss had recently defeated for president. Congressman Jack Anderson later commented, "I visited the Hoover Dam in 1933 and went all through it just about the time it was ready for completion and just before they turned the water into the penstocks. I always felt when Roosevelt and Ickes took down the plaque which dedicated the dam to Hoover--to whom it was originally dedicated--that a great injustice had been done to a great American, so I bided my time, hoping that the opportunity would arise when I could rectify what I considered a gross error. Well, in the 80th Congress, as you know -- that's the only Congress in which the Republicans controlled the House and the Senate out of the fourteen years that I served -- I decided it was time to introduce a bill to restore the name 'Hoover' to the then Boulder Dam." Anderson succeeded, and the name was changed back in 1947.

Ickes

Of course, the name meant little to those working on the project itself; they were far more preoccupied with staying on schedule. The government's contract with the Six Companies stated that the diversion tunnels had to be completed and the river moved by the end of October 1934 or the companies would be fined. As worker Tommy Nelson remembered, "The Six Companies foremen, they were on me all the time. Keep the trucks movin', everybody movin'. I was the flagman, flaggin' dump trucks. And lo and behold I took a look up, and saw a high scaler way up high on the Nevada side comin' down, and he fell very close to where I was standing. So I take a quick look, thinking that there's no trucks coming, and make a mad dash over to this guy. There's nothin' I can do for him. Along comes a hard-boiled superintendent, and I told him there's a man killed over there. And he said to me, in no uncertain terms, 'What are you going to do with all these blankety-blank trucks? Eat 'em? Get the trucks moving! He can't hurt anybody.'"

Completed tunnel lining at intake portal of diversion tunnel No. 4, looking toward entrance. Pressure for grouting jumbo seen in operation.

By May 1932, the tunnels to divert the mighty Colorado River were complete, thanks in large part to a giant device known as a drilling jumbo, which consisted of three levels of drills mounted on a 10 ton truck. When it was time to dig, the men carefully backed the truck up to the wall they were blasting and used the 30 drills to drive holes into the rock. They then placed dynamite in the completed holes and drove the drilling jumbo away to the next area. W. A. Davis explained, "That was a pretty clever idea. Because before, they'd have to put up staging. Then the staging would have to be taken down when they blew the face. And then they'd have to replace it. It was a big time saver." When Wilbur asked him how smooth the tunnels were,

Crowe proudly boasted, "As smooth as a schoolmarm's leg, Mr. Wilbur, and if I remember my geography that's pretty smooth."

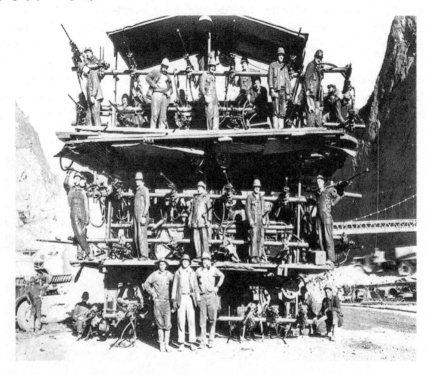

Workers on a drilling jumbo used to drill the tunnels

Of course, the drilling jumbo was hardly the only piece of specialized equipment used to build the dam. According to one author writing in 1933, "The biggest trucks in the world had to be designed and built by Mack. Powered with 250-horsepower motors and equipped with special duralumin bodies, they are capable of waddling away with sixteen cubic yards of earth–just twice the capacity of the biggest truck hitherto. Babcock & Wilcox of Barberton, Ohio, is building $10,908,000 worth of piping at a special plant erected one mile from the dam site. A General Electric unit will X-ray every inch of welding in the two and eight-tenths miles of penstocks (giant pipes carrying water from dam to power house). This world's record X-ray job involves 159,000 separate pictures and 24,000,000 square inches of film-a prodigious guaranty of welding quality. The government cableway which spans the abyss has five times the capacity of any earlier cableway. Built by Ledgerwood Manufacturing Co. of Elizabeth, New Jersey, it has six steel ropes bigger than the average man's wrist (three and one-half inches diameter) and can lower 150 tons of concrete or steel hundreds of feet from the upper workings to the pit. Engineers say it could take 200 tons or more. The roller cradle which runs along the cable dangling these crushing weights is as big as a box car. The turbines and generators for the power plant are also the largest to date: four of the turbines, contracted for by Allis-Chalmers, will turn up 115,000 horsepower apiece. The fifty-foot diversion tunnels dwarf New York's subway tubes. Fantastic machines called Jumbos run on rails into these tunnels. One has thirty-two air drills to perforate the rock; another has seven platforms, like the carriages on a ferris wheel, and carries the men who trim the walls after the rock has been blasted out; another lines the walls with. concrete--an eighty-foot section at a stop."

Even after the tunnels were completed, however, it took another year of backbreaking work to actually change the river's course from its accustomed banks to the concrete and steel tunnels. On April 23, 1933, reporters and photographers came from around the country to witness the great event. According to Nelson, "At 11:30 in the morning, a blast was put off down there, near the entry, in one of the big diversion tunnels. That was what put the show on the road." One historian explained, "Throughout the day, workers furiously dumped tons of rock into the river's path, trying to build a barrier high enough and strong enough to push it back into the tunnels. By dawn, the battle was won. Man had moved the mighty Colorado from the bed it had known for 12 million years. For Frank Crowe, it was a personal triumph — he had beaten the river, and his deadline, by eleven months." Ila Clements-Davey recalled, "The men were just swarming over the whole place, they just looked like a hill of ants they really did. It was just fantastic to watch all that going on. It was a monumental task."

Once the river was out of the way, the work began to go very quickly. The high-scalers went to work, dangling from ropes 800 feet above the ground and drilling into the sides of the canyon left behind with jackhammers, all while also using dynamite to blast out bigger chunks of rock. Clements-Davey described the scene: "It was like a movie of Tarzan, you know. You'd hear the blast and then see those guys fling themselves down there and start ripping the rocks off and there were people above them and people below them." Likewise, Maxine Riepen, who worked as a secretary for the company, said, "I remember this big, strong-looking man fell. And, uh, he yelled as he fell and this high-scaler below him swung out and caught him as he was falling and saved his life. Oh, he got write-ups and was quite a hero after that. Others... there were two or three that fell to their death. Maybe even more."

Pictures of "high-scalers" drilling into the canyon high above the river

Time was money, and by the end of 1933, the Six Companies were ahead by two years and $3 million, but under Ickes, the Six Companies were forced to integrate their formerly all-white force, and eventually, black workers came to make up a significant percentage of the 4,000 men working on the project at any given time. However, even Ickes was not about to insist that these men be allowed to move their families into Boulder City. As Clements-Davey put it, "This was a closed community. Negroes were not, there was no way a Negro could get in here. No way anyone with a colored skin could get in here."

June 6, 1933 was a monumental day as the first bucket of concrete was poured into the canyon. By this time, there were 5,000 men working on the project, all supervised by Crowe, and under his direction, multiple cables were strung up around the site to carry concrete from place to place. When working at capacity, these cables could deliver a 20 ton bucket of concrete where it was needed every 78 seconds.

Of course, this was incredibly dangerous work, and one worker, John Cahlan, told a story about it with the callousness of a man who had seen too much suffering: "[One man] was riding a -- they had these big cableways across the top of the canyon that were used to lower and raise the buckets of cement that went down. The cement plants were up on top of the canyon, and they would lower the batches of cement down by these huge buckets. They were on a big hook, and they'd just lower 'em right down from the top of the canyon. And the guys used to ride these -- ride the hook up and down and pay no attention to it. It's just like construction on some of these skyscrapers. They never think anything of riding those hooks. This fellow was on with a big bucket of cement. They were about -- oh, they just started in to drop when the hook broke. As he was going down, he waved to the boys goodbye, and they dug him out of about four or five feet of dirt. He hit down at the bottom of the canyon, and just dug a big hole in there. They finally got him, but he, as I say, he never wavered for a moment. He was just wavin' the boys goodbye!"

Pictures of the dam's columns being gradually filled with concrete

Anyone who has seen photos of the dam notices that it is not one solid wall of concrete. Had the builders tried to pour such a wall, it would still be dry today over 75 years later. Instead, they created 5 foot tall blocks that were then stacked together in an interlocking pattern until they reached the top of the dam.   Under Crowe's careful direction, and with his enthusiastic support, the crew poured the last bucket of concrete needed to complete the 72 story-tall dam on February 6, 1935. By the time it was complete, the Hoover Dam was over 720 feet tall, over 1,200 feet long, and over 650 feet wide at its base.

The Dam's Legacies

A memorial at the site commemorating those who died working on the Hoover Dam

"It is in these matters of personnel, organization, and efficiency rather than in miracles of machinery that Boulder Dam is unique in engineering history. No problems have arisen which have not been solved before on other dams. The machines differ from previous ones principally in their gigantic size. … Many of the tools in Black Canyon are on a similar scale, too big and too complicated for the layman to grasp without extensive comparative pictures and diagrams. But the engineers are modestly positive on one point: among the dam's legacies to the world will be numbered no new machine device. No puzzles of construction or design have faced them that have not been solved before. The major problem has been the job's brutal size." – Excerpt from a 1933 article in *Fortune*

Just a few days after the last concrete was poured, the gates on the diversion tunnel were closed and the mighty Colorado began to feed a new lake, Lake Mead, which quickly became the largest manmade reservoir on the planet. When full, it covered about 250 square miles and was 500 feet deep. Clements-Davey remembered, "We got into what I call now the little puddle that was the lake at that time, and we went up to the back part of the dam and this great big structure this, oh my God… big hunk of concrete, corkin' up the Colorado River. And the intake towers sitting on the cliffs, way up above us. Now when you go over the dam it looks like the intake towers are right in the middle of the lake, you know, and, and the dam, you only see a small portion of it. You can't get the feeling of the immensity of the dam, and it looks a lot bigger from that side then it does from the face side. It really does."

A picture of Lake Mead beginning to fill in against the Hoover Dam

Indeed, the look of the dam had always been a priority among its designers. According to an article which appeared in *Reclamation Era*, the magazine of the Reclamation Commission, "Probably the most significant and appropriate innovation is the selection of the decorative motifs and color scheme of our southwestern Indians as the basis of all decoration at the dam. These motifs or patterns and the distinctive color palette are eminently appropriate as well as beautifully adapted to the purpose. In the pottery designs, basketry patterns, and sand paintings of the Colorado River watershed there exists a wealth of wholly untouched and magnificent source of material….With aboriginal directness these forms are derived from stepped mesas, rain, lightning, and louds…from lizards, plumed serpents, and birds…and the fertility of invention with which these native forms and abstractions are assembled seems unlimited. The bold, frank appositions of form or color and the novelty of application or use give them a quality all their own. For character, style, and distinction there is nothing to compare with them, and their inherent boldness makes them peculiarly adaptable for use in connection with modern architecture."

The exterior of the dam was not the only area that received careful design and decoration. According to the article, "a design [is] to be executed in dull green and black terrazzo for the lobby floor of the elevator towers at the top of the dam. The walls of these lobbies are to be of highly polished black marble and the ceilings of the most modern…treated aluminum with concealed lighting.   The doors are of verdigris bronze which accords with the note of green and somber shade which is dictated by the need for a cool effect when arriving in the lobbies from the blazing heat of the dam crest. The floor design itself is an adaptation of two Pima basket patterns adjusted in scale…to the requirements of the space and location.   A little study of its central portion will reveal its striking similarity to what might be termed an engineer's basic diagram of a generator or turbine, with valves, gates, and a suggestion of centrifugal motion. What basic motif could be more appropriate or better adapted?"

September 30, 1935 was set aside as the date for the dam's dedication, and on that day, 20,000 people came to Nevada to see what a number of newspapers were already calling the 8th wonder of the world. President Roosevelt himself came to the dam to dedicate it, and in prepared remarks, he said:

> "This morning I came, I saw and I was conquered, as everyone would be who
> sees for the first time this great feat of mankind.
>
> We are here to celebrate the completion of the greatest dam in the world, rising
> 726 feet above the bedrock of the river and altering the geography of a whole
> region; we are here to see the creation of the largest artificial lake in the world—
> 115 miles long, holding enough water, for example, to cover the State of
> Connecticut to a depth of ten feet; and we are here to see nearing completion a
> power house which will contain the largest generators yet installed in this country.
>
> All these dimensions are superlative. They represent and embody the
> accumulated engineering knowledge and experience of centuries; and when we
> behold them it is fitting that we pay tribute to the genius of their designers. We
> recognize also the energy, resourcefulness and zeal of the builders, who, under the
> greatest physical obstacles, have pushed this work forward to completion two years
> in advance of the contract requirements. But especially, we express our gratitude to
> the thousands of workers who gave brain and brawn to this great work of
> construction.
>
> We know that, as an unregulated river, the Colorado added little of value to the

region this dam serves. When in flood the river was a threatening torrent. In the dry months of the year it shrank to a trickling stream. The gates of these great diversion tunnels were closed here at Boulder Dam last February. In June a great flood came down the river. It came roaring down the canyons of the Colorado, through Grand Canyon, Iceberg and Boulder Canyons, but it was caught and safely held behind Boulder Dam.

Across the San Jacinto Mountains southwest of Boulder Dam, the cities of Southern California are constructing an aqueduct to cost $220,000,000, which they have raised, for the purpose of carrying the regulated waters of the Colorado River to the Pacific Coast 259 miles away.

Across the desert and mountains to the west and south run great electric transmission lines by which factory motors, street and household lights and irrigation pumps will be operated in Southern Arizona and California.

Boulder Dam and the powerhouses together cost a total of $108,000,000. The price of Boulder Dam during the depression years provided [work] for 4,000 men, most of them heads of families, and many thousands more were enabled to earn a livelihood through manufacture of materials and machinery.

And this picture is true on different scales in regard to the thousands of projects undertaken by the Federal Government, by the States and by the counties and municipalities in recent years.

Throughout our national history we have had a great program of public improvements, and in these past two years all that we have done has been to accelerate that program. We know, too, that the reason for this speeding up was the need of giving relief to several million men and women whose earning capacity had been destroyed by the complexities and lack of thought of the economic system of the past generation.

In a little over two years this great national work has accomplished much. We have helped mankind by the works themselves and, at the same time, we have created the necessary purchasing power to throw in the clutch to start the wheels of what we call private industry. Such expenditures on all of these works, great and small, flow out to many beneficiaries; they revive other and more remote industries and businesses. Labor makes wealth. The use of materials makes wealth. To employ workers and materials when private employment has failed is to translate into great national possessions the energy that otherwise would be wasted. Boulder Dam is a splendid symbol of that principle. The mighty waters of the Colorado were running unused to the sea. Today we translate them into a great national possession.

Today marks the official completion and dedication of Boulder Dam. This is an engineering victory of the first order—another great achievement of American resourcefulness, American skill and determination.

That is why I have the right once more to congratulate you who have built Boulder Dam and on behalf of the Nation to say to you, 'Well done.'"

While the men were officially finished with the dam, it was not finished with them. In an eerie coincidence worthy of *Ripley's Believe It or Not*, Patrick Tierney slipped and fell into an intake tower on December 20, 1935, and he drowned before he could be rescued, thereby becoming the final fatality in the dam's construction. What gave so many people shivers was that he died exactly 13 years to the day after his father, surveyor J.G. Tierney, had become the project's first casualty after drowning on site. As a result, of the over 100 people to die working on the Hoover Dam, father and son were the project's first and last fatalities.

A 1998 picture of the Hoover Dam releasing water from the jet-flow gates

A modern view of the Hoover Dam

Further Reading

The Transcontinental Railroad

Andrist, Ralph K. *The Long Death: The Last Days of the Plains Indian.* New York: Collier Books, 1964.

Bain, David Haward. *Empire Express: Building the First Transcontinental Railroad.* New York: Penguin Putnam Books, 1999.

Gordon, Sarah H. *Passage to Union: How the Railroads Transformed American Life, 1829-1929.* Chicago: Elephant Paperbacks, 1997.

Griswold, Wesley S. *A Work of Giants: Building the First Transcontinental Railroad.* New York: McGraw-Hill, 1967.

Klein, Maury. *Union Pacific: Birth of a Railroad, 1862-1893*. Garden City, NY: Doubleday & Company, 1987.

Kraus, George. *High Road to Promontory: Building the Central Pacific Across the High Sierra*. Palo Alto, CA: American West Publishing Company, 1969.

Lavender, David. *The Great Persuader: The Biography of Collis P. Huntington*. Niwot, CO: University Press of Colorado, 1970.

The Panama Canal

Bennett, Ira E. *History of the Panama Canal: Its Construction and Builders*. Washington, D.C.: Historical Pub., 1915.

Cameron, Ian. *The Impossible Dream: The Building of the Panama Canal*. London: Hodder & Stoughton, 1971.

Conniff, Michael L. *Black Labor on a White Canal: Panama, 1904-1981*. Pittsburgh: University of Pittsburgh, 1985.

Greene, Julie. *The Canal Builders: Making America's Empire at the Panama Canal*. New York: Penguin, 2009.

LeFeber, Walter. *The Panama Canal: A Crisis in Historical Perspective*. New York: Oxford UP, 1989.

Lewis, Lancelot S. *The West Indian in Panama: Black Labor in Panama, 1850-1914*. Washington, D.C.: University of America, 1980.

McCullough, David G. *The Path Between the Seas: The Creation of the Panama Canal, 1870-1914*. New York: Simon and Schuster, 1977.

McGuinness, Aims. *Path of Empire: Panama and the California Gold Rush*. Ithaca: Cornell UP, 2008.

Newton, Velma. *The Silver Men: West Indian Labour Migration to Panama, 1850-1914*. Kingston, Jamaica: Ian Randle, 2004.

Otis, Fessenden N. *History of the Panama Railroad....* New York: Harper, 1867.

Panama Canal Museum. *Write of Passage: Stories of the American Era of the Panama Canal*. Seminole, FL: Rose Printing, 2008.

Parker, Matthew. *Panama Fever: The Epic Story of One of the Greatest Human Achievements of All Time -- The Building of the Panama Canal.* New York: Doubleday, 2007.

Sibert, William L., and John F. Stevens. *The Construction of the Panama Canal.* New York: D. Appleton, 1915.

Snapp, Jeremy Sherman. *Destiny by Design: The Construction of the Panama Canal.* Lopez Island, WA: Pacific Heritage, 2000.

Van Hardeveld, Rose Mahr. *Make the Dirt Fly!.* Hollywood, CA: Pan, 1956.

The Hoover Dam

Bureau of Reclamation (2006). *Reclamation: Managing Water in the West: Hoover Dam.* US Department of the Interior.

Dunar, Andrew J.; McBride, Dennis (2001) [1993]. *Building Hoover Dam: An Oral History of the Great Depression.* Reno, Nev.: University of Nevada Press.

Hiltzik, Michael A. (2010). *Colossus: Hoover Dam and the Making of the American Century.* New York: Free Press.

Stevens, Joseph E. (1988). *Hoover Dam: An American Adventure.* Norman, OK: University of Oklahoma Press.

The Story of the Hoover Dam. Las Vegas: Nevada Publications, Inc. 2006.

Free Books by Charles River Editors

We have brand new titles available for free most days of the week. To see which of our titles are currently free, click on this link.

Discounted Books by Charles River Editors

We have titles at a discount price of just 99 cents everyday. To see which of our titles are currently 99 cents, click on this link.

Made in United States
Orlando, FL
13 November 2023

38917616R00075